LETTERS FROM "APARTHEID STREET"

Letters from
"Apartheid Street"

A Christian Peacemaker in Occupied Palestine

Michael T. McRay

Foreword by Lee C. Camp

Tim —
I wrote this with a love of stories,
people, imagination, + justice. It was a
pivotal time in the journey of my faith +
spirituality. I am deeply honored + humbled
to hear it is playing a role in yours.
Much peace,

CASCADE *Books* · Eugene, Oregon

LETTERS FROM "APARTHEID STREET"
A Christian Peacemaker in Occupied Palestine

Cascade Books
An Imprint of Wipf and Stock Publishers
199 W. 8th Ave., Suite 3
Eugene, OR 97401

www.wipfandstock.com

ISBN 13: 978-1-62032-625-1

Cataloging-in-Publication data:

McRay, Michael T.

Letters from "Apartheid Street" : a Christian peacemaker in occupied Palestine / Michael T. McRay.

xxviii + 140 p. ; 23 cm. — Includes bibliographical references.

ISBN 13: 978-1-62032-625-1

1. Arab-Israeli conflict. 2. Palestinian Arabs—Israel. 3. Jewish-Arab relations. I. Title.

DS113.7 M35 2013

Excerpt from "We Teach Life" by Rafeef Ziadah is used with permission.
All Scripture references taken from New International Version (NIV).
All maps were created and used with permission by UN OCHA oPt
(www.ochaopt.org)

Manufactured in the U.S.A.

To my parents, David and Joan—
Whose abundant love and unfailing generosity
made this possible in every way

Reader Reviews

"OUR FIELD NEEDS PASSIONATE, on-the-ground, first-hand descriptions of the challenges of constructively engaging settings of deep and painful conflict. McRay's book provides just such a window."

— JOHN PAUL LEDERACH, Professor of International Peacebuilding, Joan B. Kroc Institute at the University of Notre Dame, author of numerous titles, including *When Blood and Bones Cry Out*, *The Moral Imagination*, *Building Peace*, and *Preparing for Peace*

"As a Palestinian Christian peace worker, I've learned that to truthfully and authentically do human rights work halfway across the world, we have to simultaneously reach much closer to home, into our own hearts. Michael's reflections into his internal struggles as a Christian international peace worker, intertwined with the external struggles of facing Israel's Occupation, are an important read for human rights workers who want to do this work with integrity, but more importantly, who want to learn how to be the change that they want to see in the world."

— TAREK ABUATA, Palestine Support Team Coordinator, Christian Peacemaker Teams

"Reading *Letters from 'Apartheid Street'* is a way of entering contemporary Jewish life from its most disturbing angle—the oppression of the Palestinian people. What is hopeful about these letters is the humanity the author shows through his interaction with Jews and Palestinians. In a down to earth yet profound way, this book shows Jews a way out of the injustice of occupying another people. What more important lesson do we Jews have to learn before it is too late?"

> — MARC H. ELLIS, Jewish theologian, University Professor of Jewish Studies, Baylor University, author of *Toward a Jewish Theology of Liberation* and *Judaism Does Not Equal Israel*

"I had the chance to visit Christian Peacemaker Teams in Hebron a few years before Michael McRay lived and worked there. I remember many things about my visit—dead birds stuck in razor wire, trash dropped by settlers on Palestinians, tension everywhere, guns mounted on rooftops, stern soldiers, caring and resolute CPT members, more tension. Reading Michael's poignantly-written journal of his time there showed me layers and depths that I sensed in my half-day there . . . but never could have plumbed without his on-the-ground experience and insight. A valuable resource for all who are called to be peacemakers—which should mean all of us."

> — BRIAN D. MCLAREN, speaker and author of numerous titles, including *A New Kind of Christianity, A Generous Orthodoxy,* and *Everything Must Change* (brianmclaren.net)

"While reading Michael McRay's powerful book, I could not help but recall the words Mark Twain spoke to Dan Beard regarding Twain's classic text, *The War Prayer*: 'None but the dead are permitted to tell the truth.' Therefore, Twain told Beard, his text rejecting war could be published only after he was dead. In a book at least as powerful as Twain's *War Prayer*, McRay tells the unvarnished and deeply disturbing truth regarding the Israeli occupation of Palestine—the truth he has witnessed with his own two eyes while working with Christian Peacemaker Teams in that occupied country. But McRay is not afraid of death, having exposed himself to the threat of violence and death time and again as he has sought 'to be owned' by 'the stories from below,' as he so graphically puts it. Here is a book as unflinchingly faithful to the Christian gospel as a book can possibly be."

> — RICHARD T. HUGHES, Director, Sider Institute for Anabaptist, Pietist, and Wesleyan Studies, Messiah College, and author of *Myths America Lives By* and *Christian America and the Kingdom of God*

"Michael McRay's *Letters from 'Apartheid Street'* is surprisingly invitational. I found myself wanting to walk alongside him, yearning to learn from the freshness and honesty that his stories convey. This is a book worth reading and rereading. As a guide for activism, I hope these reflections will have a profoundly rippling effect."

— KATHY KELLY, co-coordinator of Voices for Creative Nonviolence, Nobel Peace Prize nominee

"Pay serious heed to Michael McRay. In his lively commitment to actually follow the example of Jesus, he brings personal tales of wit, poetic thinking, and ethical improvisation to a world all too willing to reduce the revolutionist of Nazareth to a kind of ghost friend who mostly serves to forgive us our private sins and leave our politics untouched and unrepentant. McRay's witness demonstrates what it might mean to make Jesus lord over all we see and do and to let the whole of God's kingdom come to our sisters and brothers on all sides of our idolatrous, nationalistic divisions."

— DAVID DARK, author of *The Sacredness of Questioning Everything*, *The Gospel According to America*, and *Everyday Apocalypse*

"This is a fresh, lucid, eminently readable 'journal' of a young man's encounter with the violence of a military occupation few of us will ever see. Written 'as it happened' from his day-to-day experiences, McRay invites us to look over his shoulder as he walks down some of the most dangerous streets in the West Bank. The millions of tourists who come to Israel never visit Hebron. And the hundreds who have the courage to do so never see the things that happen behind the scenes. McRay takes us there and we watch and listen as innocence is lost and the reality of this world settles on his pen. He shows how each of us has life-shaping stories. In fact, we are drawn to stories. We shape our worldview through stories. But in this case, he wants us to hear one that we've never heard, one that will surely change how we see one city stuck in the middle of an intractable, merciless international conflict. This book is highly recommended and is sure to be well received."

— GARY M. BURGE, Professor of New Testament, Wheaton College, author of *Whose Land? Whose Promise?* and *Jesus and the Land*

"Suffering matters. Justice matters. Hope matters. Stories matter. This book matters because it has real stories that show true suffering, hope, and longing for justice and peace—borne from the depths of experience and reflection. It will serve us well to listen closely."

— PAUL ALEXANDER, Professor of Christian Ethics and Public Policy, Palmer Theological Seminary, Eastern University, author of *Peace to War*

"Compelling, honest, and engrossing. McRay is courageously touching upon one of the most important and painful disasters of our day. We will not see any signs of hope on terrorism and war until more attention—especially through stories like these—is drawn to this occupation. We desperately need voices like McRay's—and the examples of Palestinians and others courageously resisting the fearful spirit of occupation—to inspire conviction and counter our ignorance. We all need to catch McRay's risky spirit of engagement, empathy (for both violators and violated), and openness to the other."

— CHRIS HAW, co-author of *Jesus for President*, and author of *From Willow Creek to Sacred Heart*

"In a uniquely compassionate way and through disturbingly raw storytelling, Michael McRay's new book captures the essence of what it means to live under modern-day colonization and occupation. McRay presents us with an uncomfortable and stark choice: Will the Western church continue to hold to an 'air tight' theology which negates the Palestinian narrative and justifies Israeli exceptionalism? Or are we open to the possibility that our theology is inconsistent with the biblical revelation of a God who is 'no respecter of persons'? McRay invites us into new realms of social justice and peacemaking as he takes us up-close and personal, asking us to rethink what Jesus would do and *be* in the face of racism."

— REV. STEPHEN SIZER, founding member of the Institute for the Study of Christian Zionism, author of *Christian Zionism* and *Zion's Christian Soldiers*

"*Letters from 'Apartheid Street'* unmasks the daily bullying, abuse, and frequent violence against Palestinian families (both Christian and Muslim) living in occupied Palestine. This is a personal and passionate account, coming from the eyes and heart of a young Tennessean author who has lived among Palestinians and who has witnessed their suffering up close. As part of Christian Peacemaker Teams working in Hebron, McRay acknowledges that he too wrestles, alongside peaceful Palestinians, with how to turn the other cheek. This story provides the reader with a picture of the 'other side' of Palestinian life—a story that is not on the radar screen of most Americans, and yet it is a story that compels believers to seek an answer to the question: how does one work toward reconciliation in this occupied territory?

— KATHY PULLEY, Professor of Religious Studies, Missouri State University

"Michael McRay's diary of his months as a peace-justice advocate and witness in Palestine delivers in well-crafted and compelling prose the immediacy of a young man's passionate, intelligent reflections on the tragic and, for him, at times outrageous circumstances for the people in the Occupied Territories. Salient features of this first-person account include a vivid feel for the pathos in the daily grind of the Palestinians, a critical yet open interaction with individual Israeli soldiers, and probing self-examination of privilege and responsibility as a twenty-something Christian and U.S. citizen."

— BRUCE T. MORRILL, SJ, Malloy Chair of Catholic Studies and Professor of Theology, Vanderbilt University

"If you have ever dismissed pacifism as passive, you should read Michael McRay's Hebron journal. If you have ever presumed that Christianity is simply about an affirming personal relationship with Jesus, read Michael's journal. If you have ever imagined it easy to stand up to oppression, or thought love was naive, read Michael's journal. If you have, somehow, failed to consider such questions, stop reading these blurbs and buy this book."

— RICHARD C. GOODE, Professor of History, Lipscomb University, co-author of *Crashing the Idols* and editor of *And the Criminals With Him*

Table of Contents

Table of Contents

List of Maps

Foreword

WHEN I BEGAN MY teaching vocation here in the buckle of the Bible Belt thirteen years ago, I realized quickly that teaching theology and "Christian ethics" is a daunting task, a task freighted with possibilities for despair. So I spoke to my new colleague Richard Goode about my already developing sense of frustration.

He pointed me to two sources of encouragement: one, the agricultural metaphors scattered throughout the New Testament, in which the Apostle Paul clearly specifies our task, a simple and humble one. We are called to plow the ground, sow seed, water seed in our ministry of reconciliation. Sometimes we are but preparing ground upon which others, we trust, will sow seed. Sometimes we are privileged to water seed, seed that others have previously sown, upon ground that was previously plowed by yet others.

Two, he pointed me again to Oscar Romero, that faithful witness to the gospel who was murdered because he insistently spoke truth to oppressors and to those who thought violence more mighty than love. Romero, too, said on various occasions that liberation comes in knowing that we cannot do everything ourselves. Romero reminds us that we are only workers in God's great plans.

As one of Michael's teachers, I am grateful to say I got to water some of the seed that had already been sown by others, and I am grateful to our friends at Cascade and Wipf and Stock for bringing Michael's recounting of his experiences in Israel and Palestine to publication.

But more than that, I am grateful to see herein his own struggle to embody a life of sowing the seed of God's Kingdom. I am grateful that this journal—one which I encouraged him to seek to have published—allows us to see his own struggles. It is worth noting that even though Michael often speaks and acts boldly, he is as riddled with questions as the rest of us. So I am grateful he refuses to come to too-easy conclusions. And I am grateful for his willingness to acknowledge forthrightly that even his own peace-making work carries with it an inescapable air of white, male privilege, especially significant when carrying a U.S. passport through Palestinian checkpoints.

Embodying the gospel is not, of course, an exercise in self-righteousness. Thus these pages, perhaps *because* of the ambiguity and questions herein, bear witness to a faithful attempt to practice the Good News of a Kingdom described on the Galilean hills also described herein.

I have seen many of the streets, shops, and walls Michael describes here. I have also seen the tension between oppressor and oppressed. Those of us at ease in the American Zion must needs hear the stories: a family whose home was destroyed by heavy machinery while the family was still inside, killing children and a pregnant mother and a grandparent; olive groves, cultivated for generations, uprooted to build a wall of separation; domesticity and labor and child-rearing constantly threatened by arbitrary-but-all-too-well-imposed systems of check-points and confiscation and arrest, maddening to even the casual observer; heartless mechanisms of colonialism and occupation. I walked, some years ago, only a half-day the streets of Hebron, and only a half-day the markets of Ramallah, and only brief stints in other locales in the West Bank, and I found my anger to be boiling and accompanied with cursing. You will see the same frustration herein, and for good reason.

But it is that temptation to self-righteousness which is so dangerous: We begin to tell, as Michael so well puts it, a "single narrative," in which all the wickedness is on one side, and all the righteousness on the other. And—this is something I learned herein—we have a felt-need for a "perfect victim," the victim in whom there is no guile, before we will commit ourselves in empathy for the oppressed.

Michael's own questions and inner arguments about narrative and victim show the seed of the gospel at work in his life. In his epilogue, you will hear Michael call to mind the word of Will D. Campbell, himself angry over the death of a good young man, murdered in the height of the civil rights movement, in which we Americans struggled with our own systems of apartheid. Campbell realized that he was demonizing the white-man, the murderer. A friend, an agnostic Jew, sensing the inconsistency in

Campbell's demonization of the white racist, pushed Campbell to summarize the gospel in ten words or less. Campbell insisted that that was a useless exercise. The agnostic insisted. Campbell blurted out, "We're all bastards, but God loves us anyway."

Surely Campbell's eight-word aphorism is an insufficient summary of the gospel, but it points, nonetheless, at an indispensable truth which we must carry with us in our work of sowing and watering the seed of the gospel: we are all broken, sharing together in the woundedness of the world and the fundamental alienation that marks human history. And so you will hear herein not only tales you must be sure to hear, of the oppression of Palestinians, but the humanity of Israeli Defense Forces, nineteen- and twenty-year-olds many of whom hate, too, the drama of hostility into which they have been caught up, wanting to go home and return to their own visions of domesticity and olive trees and child-rearing. So I am very glad Michael sought to carry on conversations about tennis and celebrities and life-goals with young men carrying M16's who were doing the work of the occupying forces.

As he reflects—both in one moving account of a particular protest, complete with tear gas canisters and rubber bullets and tanks and jeeps, and also in his own epilogue—it's not always clear *why* we do such things: *why* we protest injustice; *why* we seek to make peace; *why* we bear witness to a Galilean who was also murdered in Palestine. That is, it's not clear *why* we do such things when we can see no clear fruit.

I suspect that there are at least two good reasons, and probably many more: one, our continuing to sow seed, which we cannot ensure will yield a harvest, is one way of keeping our own souls tender enough to receive in our own lives the ongoing work of God's Spirit of reconciliation and peace-making. "The life you save may be your own." And two, what else is there to do? We have heard the call of Jesus, to follow in the way of truth-telling and suffering-love and doing-justice, and to listen not to the siren song of power and might and imposition. If we are not to fall prey to the various manifestations of oppression ourselves, then all there is to do is to continue such good work, together, one day at a time, trusting that the Lord of all creation will do what is right.

Lee C. Camp

Preface

GOOD STORIES ARE LIKE rivers. On the surface, the water often seems serene and powerless. Yet, beneath this surface flows the power to sculpt canyons. Good stories have this powerless power, eroding away our facades to reveal haunting and beautiful images of what it means to be human. Other stories deceive, however, seducing us to be less than we should. Falling prey, we embrace them as truth. Whether for good or ill, however, stories shape us. They are forces that give us meaning, whispers compelling us to *go* and *do*, *stay* and *be*.

I believe stories are powerful. We own our stories, and they own us. We live within our narratives and are structured by them. I am who I am both because of the stories I choose and those that choose me. I was twelve when I saw Dachau; nineteen when I stood before the brick ovens of Auschwitz. My father told me there that whatever beliefs I held of the world or of God must make sense in *these* places or they cannot make sense at all. The stories of such places are incomprehensible, yet their impossibility forms me, calling me to action on behalf of those scarred by violence and neglect.

My travels continue to challenge me with stories that emerge from beneath the rubble of destruction and poverty. I have seen narratives of violence and neglect in the mountains of rural Appalachia, where my own story began; in the struggle for hope found in the faces of the homeless and incarcerated of Nashville, whom I am privileged to know; and in the blood-stained soil of Palestine, where I continually find myself called. I believe *these* types of stories are the most important. They are the call "from below," as German theologian Dietrich Bonhoeffer reflected in *Letters and Papers from Prison*: "We have for once learnt to see the great events of world history from below, from the perspective of the outcast, the suspects, the maltreated, the powerless, the oppressed, the reviled—in short, from the perspective of those who suffer."[1] Those living "below" have stories that frequently do not find ears that hear. I seek to train mine to listen to these stories and be owned by them so that I must live within their painful pages. The pain of these stories, compounded by the injustice embedded within them, compels me to service. Rooted in a love of people and places, I am seeking to weave my story into the human narrative's recurring patterns of violence and death by joining those seeking to sew threads of wholeness and rebirth.

My parents moved to East Tennessee immediately after my birth so my father could work with a community health center as a family physician, offering quality care to the uninsured. Intending to relocate to Central America, they instead found themselves drawn to the stories of their neighbors and his patients, and so they planted roots in that community. Just as the faces and narratives of the poor and sick of our small town altered my parents' direction and informed their story, so have the faces and narratives of the men at Nashville's Riverbend Maximum Security Institution guided mine.

I first visited the prison in late 2009, looking to serve. Yet, as several friends and I continued to go back each week, my notions of service faded as the dynamic transformed from "us" and "them" to simply "us." Our stories intertwined. Through conversation, listening, and creating the space for reconciliation, the offenders became friends, and then the friends became brothers. Our small community at Riverbend has been part of the rhythm of my life. Without it, I feel unstable. All of us are attempting to reconcile the outside world of society and the invisible world of the prison, the world which society wishes would stay "out of sight, and out of mind." Yet, we refuse to accept this, and seek to tell our brothers at Riverbend, and therefore our brothers and sisters in all prisons and behind all separation walls, that though they have been placed out of our sight, we refuse to keep them out of our minds; though the State has deemed them irrelevant to our political system, we refuse to accept them as irrelevant to our lives; and though the State has indicted them as dangerous criminals, we also see the evil in ourselves and seek to meet them in their penance so that we also may be penitent. In short, the space of stories at Riverbend is the space of crucifixion and resurrection, the space of Christ, where God is in the midst. The joining of our stories breaks down the walls the Powers use to separate

1. Bonhoeffer, *Letters and Papers from Prison*, 17, emphasis mine.

us, and it is this liberating power of stories which compels me again and again to Israel and Palestine.[2]

In early 2000, I made my first trip to Israel as a young boy, when my father, grandparents, and I ventured no farther into the West Bank than the town of Bethlehem. I returned from this trip enthralled with Israel, its culture, and Jewish heritage. During an extended family sabbatical abroad the next year, I returned for one month and my fascination with Israel deepened. Then, in 2007, several years after my father began exploring alternative stories after stumbling across literature by the Israeli human rights group B'tselem, my eyes opened to the narrative of the Palestinian people and their struggles under Israeli military occupation. Through subsequent trips and through my study of their history, I have grown to ache more deeply with those on both sides suffering from the ensuing oppressions of power and powerlessness. While volunteering in the West Bank with the Al Basma Center for the Developmentally Disabled during the summer of 2010, I looked into the eyes of Palestinians denied basic human rights and heard the stories of families devastated by the terror of violence and the endless cycles of retribution. I have heard the muffled words of those who cannot cry out from under the weight of oppression, and I yearn for peace. The stories of Israel and Palestine compel me to responsibility, blessing me with an indignation that drives me to try what many often claim cannot be done to help the suffering and the poor. I desire to dedicate myself to the work of justice, peacemaking, and reconciliation, particularly between the neighboring but alienated peoples of that war-torn land, and thus I returned in January 2012 to work with Christian Peacemaker Teams (CPT) in the major West Bank city of Hebron.

2. Regarding the Israeli-Palestinian conflict, terminology reveals much, as it can quickly indicate one's so-called sympathies. Since it is a conflict primarily over geography and resources, how one identifies the land is significant. I find it impossible to speak about the conflict (or even the place) without being political. Language *is* political. No matter which designation one chooses, someone is bound to find offense. Some prefer to call the whole land *Israel*, while others choose to acknowledge the historical Palestinian claim by referencing the *Palestinian Territories* or the *West Bank and Gaza*. Others speak proleptically, calling it *Palestine*, while others reference the *occupied territories*. Still others prefer the *administered territories* or *Judea and Samaria*. The UN officially designates the land as the *occupied Palestinian territories*. For the purposes of this book, I will use the *West Bank*, *Palestine*, and *Occupied Palestine* interchangeably, referring to all territory inside the Green Line, and recognizing of course that the hopes of a Palestinian state would also include the Gaza Strip. For a helpful map of the geography of Israel and Palestine, see the "OCCUPIED PALESTINIAN TERRITORY" map in the back of the book. This map was created by the UN OCHA oPt (www.ochaopt.org).

My draw to CPT's project in Hebron stemmed from both their location in Palestine and their commitment to nonviolent peacemaking. Attempting to incarnate a response to the question, "What would it look like if Christians devoted the same self-sacrifice and discipline to nonviolent peacemaking that soldiers devote to war?" CPT engages areas of violent conflict as it partners with locals to pursue alternatives to the normal responses of trained (and untrained) killing. I believe in their work and wanted to join. As Kentucky farmer, poet, and prophet Wendell Berry writes, after all the failed attempts at peace that nation-states have pursued, "there is one great possibility that we have hardly tried: that we can come to peace by being peaceable."[3] Disillusioned with the myth of redemptive violence, I became compelled to try peaceableness for once.

The following pages are letters full of the stories and reflections I sent back home during my three months in the West Bank. I did not write them with any publication objectives, but rather simply intended them to be updates for friends and family who were supporting me, financially or otherwise. I hoped both to provide those on the outside with insights as to the reality I was currently witnessing and had witnessed numerous times before, as well as to provide myself with an opportunity to process my experiences. Yet, with each update came replies from numerous people, including authors like Lee Camp and David Dark, encouraging me to seek publication. With continued assistance and advice from professor/author friends and mentors, this book found its way onto publishers' desks and now has emerged bound and distributed.

No doubt some will criticize these writings as being "biased and unbalanced," ignoring the Israeli story and giving all the weight and power to the Palestinian one.[4] Though moments of balanced recounting do appear in this work, the purpose of this storytelling exercise has not been to *be* balanced but rather to *provide* balance. I want to offer a different perspective from the prevailing Western narrative, to contest the dominant narrative's power by inserting a less familiar one into the reader's vision. The average reader, particularly in the United States, will likely be much more familiar with the Israeli narrative than the Palestinian. Through important films and museums, mandatory curriculums, and Western media, most are aware of

3. Berry, *Sex, Economy, Freedom, and Community*, 84.

4. Here I draw distinction between the *Israeli* and *Palestinian* narratives. Though I am well aware of the Palestinian minority in Israel, I use *Israeli* here to reference its Jewish majority.

the Jewish narrative's pages of persecution, suffering, and Holocaust, which contributed to the rise of the Israeli state in 1948. But the Palestinians have an important story as well, and it must be told. Ignoring their story gives all weight and power to one narrative, and this has dangerous repercussions.

This distinction of narrative is vitally important—that is, which among the competing narratives is being considered? One pure, uncontested narrative regarding episodes in history or current events is simply an illusion. As is often the case, history is written by the victorious and the powerful. One benefit of power is the ability to choose how one's stories are told, and thus how people remember them. If only the powerful tell the story, then the narrative of history is very particular, and from the victors' perspective, verifiable. Thus, if we continue to look at the Israeli-Palestinian conflict *exclusively* from the Israeli perspective, we will garner a very specific interpretation, which, though perhaps factual, will be terribly incomplete.[5]

To clarify, I am not attempting to argue *against* selective history or storytelling, as that would be a useless task, since such selection and emphasis is inevitable for the storyteller. We cannot hear and tell every story. When that selection occurs, however, we reveal our prejudices or ideological leanings. To tell only the stories of the powerful, the conqueror, the triumphant, is to deny the legitimacy and significance of the stories of the conquered and the oppressed. This is not to argue that storytelling should always "grieve for the victims and denounce the executioners," as the late Howard Zinn noted. Such role differentiation may sometimes prove nebulous, as can be the case regarding the Israeli-Palestinian conflict. In the end, Zinn observed, oppressors are also victims, and the victims themselves often turn on others, continuing the downward spiral of violence. Yet, Zinn noted most poignantly that though "the cry of the poor is not always just . . . if you don't listen to it, you will never know what justice is."[6]

This is the incredible importance of studying the other narrative. Such reconsideration forces redefinitions of ideas such as *justice* and *progress*. What many claim as progress in the Middle East (that is, the creation of the

---

5. For this reason, I believe that history teachers have one of the most important roles in peacemaking in our world. The stories our teachers tell us of the past inform our understanding of the possibilities for the present as well as the future. For example, we rarely are taught the rich history of nonviolent social movements, and thus we often are not able to imagine any other response but violent engagement when evil rears its ugly head. If we do not know that nonviolence *has* worked historically, we will not believe that it can work presently.

6. Zinn, *A People's History*, 11.

State of Israel) also meant the genesis of the world's largest refugee population. So the question becomes, who should determine the rightness or progressive nature of an action—the powerful and wealthy, or the powerless and the poor, those who suffer the brunt of such actions?

This is in no way attempting to delegitimize or downplay the suffering of the Jews over the last decades and centuries. The tragedy of the Holocaust speaks for itself. Rather, this is a call not to let the suffering of one people justify the suffering of another. As my brother Jonathan McRay succinctly states in his book *You Have Heard It Said*, "the Holocaust cannot justify the *Nakba* and the Occupation; the *Nakba* does not justify suicide bombings and rockets."[7] No group's suffering is more legitimate than another's. I appreciate the words of Palestinian writer Afif Safieh, who wrote:

> If I were a Jew or a Gypsy, the Holocaust would be the most horrible event in History [sic] . . . If I were a Native American, it would be the discovery of the New World by European explorers and settlers that resulted in near total extermination . . . If I happen to be Palestinian, it would be the Nakba-Catastrophe. *No one people has a monopoly on human suffering.* It is not advisable to establish a hierarchy of suffering. Humanity should consider all the above as morally repugnant and politically unacceptable.[8]

We must let down the rigid defenses of our theologies, release ourselves from the necessities of political success, and renounce the myths of "might makes right," or the same old tunes of history will keep playing back like a broken record. To acknowledge and, if we can, *embrace* "the other's" story is to give the silenced voices of history and of our world a chance to have the floor, and in the hearing of their testimonies, we must be willing to call injustice what it is, speaking with forthrightness and honest conviction. Otherwise, we have no hope of building a better future from the rubble of our past.

In short, we need to tell new stories, different stories. If stories shape us, then the stories we choose to tell, those that become the liturgy of our lives, determine our formation, the direction of our journeys, and the processes of our convictions. To tell new stories is to allow their powerless power to strip us of our prejudices and settled assessments and be transformed. Our old foundations are destroyed, and new ones are built. When

---

7. McRay, *You Have Heard It Said*, xiii. For a brief clarification of the *Nakba*, see the Glossary.

8. Quoted in Sabbagh, *Palestine*, 321, emphasis mine.

we participate in the telling of different stories, we allow some part of us to die—whether false perceptions, weak theologies, poorly formed convictions, etc.—and from this death, new life springs forth within us. Thus, storytelling can be an act of resurrection. If we heed Bonhoeffer's words to listen to the stories "from below," then the space of storytelling can become the space of loss and renewal, of death and rebirth, of transformation. But for this to happen, we must first pursue humility, for without humility, we will not have the ears to hear.

I do not know, however, whether people will truly hear the stories in this book or rather brush them aside, but I must voice them regardless. We do not *necessarily* tell our stories because we think people should hear them. Rather, sometimes we tell stories simply because we must, because they burn inside us. Good stories create an itch within that can only be alleviated through speaking, by imparting their gripping verses. I wrote these stories not only because people do *need* to hear them, but also because I am simply compelled to tell them. Silence is not an option.

These letters home remain largely unaltered, save for occasional clarification. I wanted to leave them in their original state so as to avoid the risk of inserting post-experience rationalizations and interpretations. At times, my thoughts throughout these letters may seem inconsistent, perhaps even contradictory, but this was, and remains, the nature of the journey. We are fluid creatures, always (one hopes) in a state of becoming, resisting the urge to be sedentary in our comforts and assumptions.

Perhaps more than anything, this book narrates my own personal struggles, my search for a more faithful witness to the good news of Jesus. In it resides numerous tensions, perhaps the greatest of which entails wrestling with my innate white-male privilege. As the light-colored North American son of a physician, I was born into privilege, with the resources of power always available. No matter what I do, I will always bring this identity (or at least the possibility of this identity) to the table. The assumption of privilege seems to be inherent in much of the work of international peacemaking. Embedded in such practices is an otherness from the directly-affected parties that makes such pursuits possible. All my actions in Hebron, or even in broader Palestine, were made possible by my place of privilege. My very *presence* there was an act of privilege, much like the existence of this book. Yet, I am not currently convinced that we can eliminate all privilege, nor do I know if this is necessary. To paraphrase my CPT teammate Chris, "We can't get rid of our white male privilege. Rather the question is what we will do with it." Throughout these letters, I tried to remain keenly aware of the intrinsic power of my privilege, seeking ways to resist its paternalistic tendencies. I did not always succeed, though, as some of these stories no doubt expose. Yet, I hope my incapability to remain steadfast in my convictions simply testifies to the evolving nature of the human journey.

In the end, I ask that you read these writings for what I intended them to be: a look "from below," an opportunity to hear the stories of a misunderstood and misrepresented people, and a chance to wrestle with the complex and, often, seemingly fruitless endeavor of being peaceable in a violent world.

Michael McRay
Nashville, Tennessee

1

The Beginning

Saturday, December 31, 2011—Newark, United States

I AM IN THE airport in Newark, New Jersey, sitting just outside the special Israeli security area. Israel has this type of special security in each airport offering direct flights to Tel Aviv. This security check is in addition to normal airport security. It probably goes without saying why Israel requires extra security. Security is everything in Israel. Obviously, all nation-states are concerned with security. Each wants to be safe, to protect its citizens. This is why nation-states have militaries. The logic is that the more military power one has, the safer one is from external threats. But Israel is even unique to this arguably universal standard among recognized nation-states. Given a history of persecution against the Jewish people, and in light of historical and ongoing tensions in the Middle East, Israel has understandable reason to be paranoid about its security. Double security measures are just one small indication of this paranoia. When one arrives in Tel Aviv and enters the land, one sees the way this fear has affected the whole of Israeli life, and thereupon the life of those around Israel. I hope to write more about this after I arrive.

Allow me to give a little background for this trip. I made my first trip to Israel and Palestine in 2000 with my father and his parents. The next year my entire family visited the land for a month during a six-month sabbatical, which we spent primarily in Greece. I did not return until 2007, when my father and I spent a week traveling around the West Bank and Israel making preparations for subsequent annual medical trips he now takes with med students and residents. In 2010, I spent spring break of my junior year in college attending a Christian peace conference in Bethlehem (which I will attend again this year) and visiting my brother (who was working with Musalaha[1], a reconciliation organization based in Jerusalem) and my dad (who was leading his medical group). I returned again that summer with two college friends, Jonathon Valentin and Paul Reeser, to volunteer in Beit Sahour, a small town adjacent to Bethlehem. During our two months, we worked primarily with the Al Basma Center for the Developmentally Disabled.[2] This beautiful organization was founded by a dear family friend with whom I will be staying during my week in Bethlehem for the peace conference in early March. This current trip, though, will be quite different than any of the previous ones.

I arrive in Tel Aviv tomorrow, and on Monday, I begin a two month internship with Christian Peacemaker Teams (CPT) in Hebron. As is widely known but too often denied, Israel is maintaining a military occupation in Palestine.[3] Recounting the history of the occupation and all the details of daily life for Palestinians inside what are "officially" known as the Palestinian Territories is much too large a task to do in this first update.[4] Throughout the next three months (I return to the U.S. just before Easter), I will be documenting my experiences and sharing my thoughts from my work with CPT.

As I understand it, CPT began as a call to the Mennonite Church for Christians to begin taking Jesus's teachings of nonviolence seriously. CPT holds that if Christians truly are to claim that the cross is an alternative (or perhaps *the* alternative) to the sword, then Christians must be willing to pay the price for this claim. Soldiers are willing to die by the thousands

1. For more on Musalaha, visit their website: www.musalaha.org.

2. For more on Al Basma, see Jonathan McRay's essay at the end of the book. See also a fantastic recent documentary directed by Zachary Crow called *We See No Enemy* (www.weseenoenemy.com). This highly recommended film introduces five stories from the West Bank, one of which is Al Basma, creating a kind of West Bank anthology. *We See No Enemy* includes interviews with my brother, father, and beloved family friends in Palestine.

3. That is, the West Bank and Gaza. Officially, Israel withdrew its settlers and soldiers from within Gaza in 2005, but it has maintained a blockade of the area. Israel controls all comings and goings to and from Gaza.

4. See "Further Reading" below for my recommendations on literature regarding the Israeli-Palestinian conflict.

for what they believe in; Christians must be willing to do the same. Thus, CPT has organized teams that have a permanent presence now in Palestine, Colombia, Canada, and Iraqi Kurdistan. CPT seeks to get physically in the way of violence—thus their motto: "getting in the way."[5] In Palestine, they stand alongside both nonviolent Palestinian and Israeli partners resisting violence, supporting them by sitting atop houses set to be illegally demolished, confronting soldiers who are harassing locals, and recording *everything* they see so that those on the outside can come to know the reality on the ground. This is an organization that wants to take seriously Jesus's call to "love your enemies." But Jesus knew you cannot love people you do not know. He spoke the haunting words above to a people whose enemies, internal and external, were in their midst, in their everyday lives. Jesus knew that loving your enemies means getting personal with the "other." This is certainly dangerous and terrifying, but there are incredible stories of transformation of people who refused to dehumanize, and instead acknowledged the human quality of the other, creating space for justice, reconciliation, and peacebuilding. This is what CPT seeks to be a part of.[6]

I am excited for this journey. It will be a very different experience for me, both due to the nature of the work and the fact that I am going alone, which is something I have never done in my travels to nearly thirty countries. I have always had at least one familiar face with me. For this, and many other reasons, I am nervous, but I remain hopeful for a meaningful experience.

5. For a variety of reasons, CPT has moved away from this language and instead adopted the motto: "Building partnerships to transform violence and oppression."

6. For more on CPT, visit their website: www.cpt.org.

2

Welcoming the Enemy

Thursday, January 5, 2012—Hebron, Occupied Palestine

"CPT! CPT! COME, COME! The soldiers have a man!"[1] Her voice startled me. Jean, Rosie, and I had been returning from afternoon patrol, but I had lagged behind to look at a few shops in Hebron's Old City. Though I did not know the woman requesting my presence, she knew who I was. My red hat and grey vest bearing the CPT name and logo unmistakably identify with whom I work. Her call immediately made me nervous. I was alone, inexperienced in the field. Questions flooded my mind. How do I proceed? What are CPT protocols in this situation? What do the people expect me to do? Do they really expect I can free a detained man from a group of Israeli soldiers? Despite my hesitancies, I set down the potential gift I was holding and followed the woman.

Turning a corner, I arrived on scene in a matter of seconds. Four Israeli soldiers stood in a semicircle next to a wall, with two more in the center. One was pointing a gun toward a Palestinian man who was leaning casually against the stone wall, and the other had the Palestinian's green identification card, radioing his headquarters to check the ID. Soldiers do this often, randomly check the IDs of passersby. As far as I can tell, no

---

1. Variations of this chapter have appeared at the *Tokens Show Blog*, May 31, 2012, (www.tokensshow.com/guest-blog-michael-mcray/) and CPT's website, January 5, 2012, (http://www.cpt.org/cptnet/2012/01/10/al-khalil-hebron-reflection-welcoming-enemy).

rhyme or reason exists for their method of choosing whom to check. The superior gives the command to check IDs, so they check IDs. While some may excuse the soldiers since they are ostensibly only "following orders," the Palestinians do not share that sentiment. They feel harassed. For the soldiers, it is of no real importance the agenda of the Palestinian, his or her errand or timeframe. If a soldier wants to check an ID, then the Palestinian must stand there and wait. This particular man was not even crossing a checkpoint. He was merely walking through the old *suuq* (marketplace) of his city, just like everyone else. Palestinians can generally be held for ID checks for as long as twenty minutes before calls and interventions are made, which often are ineffective. This is no doubt a major inconvenience for the people.

I was unsure of how to proceed. This being only my second day on team, I had not yet encountered any incidents I could use as reference points. I tried calling Jean, but quickly remembered her phone was charging and thus not with her. I accepted the fact I was on my own for this one. I decided to do what I had always read that CPTers do: that is, confront the soldiers.

"Why are you holding this man," I said to one of the soldiers in the middle. "What did he do?" No answer. "Why do you need to check his ID?" The soldier looked up at my eyes with seeming disdain but said nothing. I turned to the man pointing the gun at the detainee. "Why are you pointing a gun at him? What did he do?" Still no response from anyone.

Realizing I would not get the soldiers to talk to me, I decided to at least make them aware that I was documenting their actions. I pulled out my small blue notebook and transcribed the scene. My hands shook as I began photographing and videoing. I had never before confronted someone carrying an automatic weapon, much less six people. After only a few minutes, however, the ID cleared, and the soldiers released the Palestinian. Both parties proceeded about their business.

I decided to follow the soldiers, though, to see if they stirred up any other mischief. Trailing them by only a few feet, I held my camera up, videoing their march. They walked in two lines, three to a line, and seemed to be practicing some kind of drill or routine. Periodically, a couple would lift up their rifles, briefly taking aim at houses above, or down alleyways. After the first one pointed his weapon, the soldier(s) behind him followed suit. I could not determine any purpose to this march.

As they approached the end of the Old City, one of the soldiers in the back turned and quickly pointed the barrel of his weapon into an elderly man's shop. This was the first time I had seen a soldier point a gun in a shop. The store owner sat out in front, his head just beneath the level of the gun's barrel. Given the larger situation, I assumed the man would protest, sharing some choice words with this occupier who was arbitrarily directing his weapon into the man's place of business. But the man did not. He simply bowed his head, lifted his hand, palm upwards, and said, "*Ahlan wasahlan*, you are most welcome."[2] His response so caught me off guard I laughed out loud. Here was an Israeli soldier—a member of the military occupying this Palestinian man's land, a representation of the occupation itself—who walks the streets of Hebron to protect the Israeli settlers who illegally take more and more land from this man and his people. In short, there walked his enemy. And this Arab Muslim man extended his hand in humble invitation.

Resistance. *Al-Hamdililah*, thanks be to God.

---

2. See the Glossary for an elaboration of the phrase's meaning.

3

Life On Team

Sunday, January 8, 2012—Hebron, Occupied Palestine

THE WEEK IS OVER. A new work week begins today (since this is a Muslim city, Sunday is not a day off). I am growing accustomed to the routine of team life. When I arrived, I joined three others on team: Kathy, Jean, and Rosie. Kathy is the resident expert on CPT Palestine. She was on the survey team that first visited Hebron in 1993, and, save for a five-year period when she was denied entry, she has visited Hebron every year since. She is gentle, energetic, and cares as much for the Palestinian people as anyone I have met. Jean is a CPT reservist, a member of the Sisters of Maryknoll community in New York, and is 81 years old. She is vibrant and assertive, and has no tolerance for injustice. After fifty years working in Japan, Jean joined CPT and has served on the Palestine team off and on since 2007. Rosie is a member of a missionary community in Canada, spent twenty-eight years in Nigeria, and is a passionate, kindhearted, eager 70 year-old woman. She arrived in Palestine for the first time in November and was scheduled to leave at the end of December, but volunteered to stay another month to help out the team as we are low in numbers. On Thursday, our fifth member arrived. Chris is 30 years old, a full-time CPTer, and on his first trip to Palestine. Chris has spent the last three years working with CPT in Colombia, and spent four years before that living in a Catholic Worker house in Cleveland. I am quite pleased with the team and am enjoying working with such fascinating and experienced individuals. I have much to learn from their wisdom.

We hold to a fairly repetitive routine here. Sunday through Thursday, we have early morning school patrol. We station ourselves at two different checkpoints, one at the Ibrahimi Mosque (which houses the Tomb of the Patriarchs—the traditional burial site of Abraham, Sarah, Isaac, Jacob, Rebecca, and Leah), and one at a place called Qeitun, a five-minute walk from the mosque.[1] Our main tasks here are to count the number of children that pass through the checkpoint (numbers that go to the UN), observe how many children's bags are searched (which is *not* supposed to happen), as well as note whether teachers' IDs are checked, if any body searches are conducted, or any other noteworthy incidents.

Today, for instance, I was stationed at Qeitun with Benjamin Krauss, a young German visitor from Tent of Nations.[2] The soldiers at the checkpoint must have received an order to begin checking the IDs of the *shebaab* (younger men, generally between 16 and 40) because in the middle of our patrol, the soldiers suddenly began detaining young men at the checkpoint. They held seven men, probably in their early to mid-twenties, for just under ten minutes as they checked their IDs. One Palestinian in particular visibly expressed his frustration through his body language. He had not even been passing through the checkpoint, but the soldiers called him over anyway and made him give up his ID so they could check it. After seven or eight minutes, they asked him to go around the road block and enter through the metal detectors inside the checkpoint corridor. He argued with them briefly, clearly frustrated that he had to pass through the metal detectors when he was not crossing the checkpoint in the first place. Knowing he would not win the battle, he passed through the metal detector, but the soldiers made him go back through and take off his belt. Finally, nearly fifteen minutes after being stopped, they let him leave.

At another point, one of the soldiers unstrapped his automatic weapon from his back and held it in his hand, like a handgun. He then entered the corridor where three young Palestinian schoolboys stood, waiting to exit. The door closed behind him. I moved my position so I could see through the glass of the door, and I saw him standing over the boys, weapon in

1. For a better understanding of the geography of Hebron, see "WEST BANK CLO-SURE—HEBRON H2 AREA" map in the back of the book. This map was created by UN OCHA oPt (www.ochaopt.org).

2. For more on the incredible work of Tent of Nations, visit their website: www.tentofnations.org.

hand. I do not know what was said, but I am confident he had no legitimate reason for engaging them the way he did. When they came out, I asked them, "*Qwayes*? Good?" They nodded and ran on to school. Another Palestinian man at the Ibrahimi Mosque was detained for over forty-five minutes while they checked his ID. He was clearly in a hurry, and had to make several phone calls to apologize for his tardiness. He seemed to be in some kind of trouble for missing an appointment, as he tried to explain over the phone that he had no control over the situation. This is daily routine for Palestinians.

Aside from these checkpoint patrols, we also visit Al-Bweireh, an area on the edge of Hebron that neighbors an Israeli settlement. For those unaware of the term *settlement*, it refers to Israeli communities that have been illegally built on Palestinian land inside the 1967 borders. To be brief, Palestinians (and a number of Jews as well) lived on all this land for centuries before 1948. In the late 1800s and early 1900s, Jewish immigration significantly increased with the creation of a political movement in Europe known as Zionism, led by the Hungarian-born Jewish journalist Theodor Herzl. The United Nations found it necessary to partition the land in 1947 between the Zionist Jewish minority and the indigenous Palestinian majority, with the Jewish population receiving more land than the Palestinians. The Zionists accepted partition, while the Palestinians did not. In May 1948, the Zionist leadership declared independence from Britain (who occupied the land at the time) and established the State of Israel. War then broke out between the surrounding Arab nations and the new Zionist state. This war played a major role in the displacement of approximately 750,000 Palestinians. Israel won the war and expanded the partition lines, maintaining the new borders for nearly twenty years. Then in 1967, Israel, believing in an imminent attack from their Arab neighbors, launched a preemptive strike on the surrounding Arab nations and defeated them all in what is known as the Six-Day War. At this point, Israel began its current occupation of the West Bank and Gaza, taking them from Jordan and Egypt, respectively. The borders between Israel and its neighbors that existed before the 1967 war are known as the Green Line or the 1967 borders. They are the only internationally recognized borders between Israel and the West Bank. Any Israeli towns or cities, then, built on the Palestinian side of the Green Line since 1967 are considered illegal under international law, have been condemned in numerous UN resolutions, and are probably the single greatest hindrance to any type of peace agreement.[3]

The settlement at Al-Bweireh poses a major problem for the Palestinians there. The IDF (Israeli military) has blocked the Palestinian road that runs near the settlement, prohibiting parents from driving their children to school.[4] The children therefore must walk beside the settlement every day to attend school. Because young settlers often attack the children with rocks, CPT and other protective presence organizations escort those children along the road to guard them from the stone throwing and other methods of settler attacks. One Palestinian family lives directly adjacent to the settler Outpost 26 and frequently experiences settler attacks of rock throwing at their home. These rocks break their windows, destroy their solar panels, and keep the family living in fear. CPT occasionally stays the night with the family on Fridays and/or Saturdays, the days when the attacks usually occur.

One of CPT's closest and oldest Palestinian friends here, Hanna, lives on Tel Rumeida, a hill in Hebron that settlers have almost completely taken over.[5] His family owned good land which produced excellent grapes, walnuts, and olives. They exported these and made a very sufficient income. As is expected, the settlers want his land and have offered him millions of dollars for it. But he continues to refuse. His family has no desire to leave. As punishment, the settlers, using a kind of homemade napalm, have torched and poisoned his land, destroyed his tools for farming, and continually burned his cars (his family is currently on their *eighth* one). Nothing grows on his land now. He told us, "I used to make much money from exporting the olives I grew. This year, I *bought* all of them." When asked if he thinks the building of the settlements will ever stop, he responded with a laugh, "Let them build the settlements! For me, this is no problem. We have many Palestinian refugees who will need good housing when they return!" I am shocked at his positive outlook given the gravity of his circumstances. I hope to learn from this.

3. Please see the end of the book for "Restricting Space in the oPt: Area C Map," created by the UN OCHA oPt (www.ochaopt.org). All areas controlled by the settlements and Israeli military are highlighted.

4. *IDF* stands for Israeli Defense Forces. Many locals, however, refer to the army as the IOF, Israeli Occupation Forces, since they argue military presence in the West Bank has little do with national defense and everything to do with occupation.

5. Hanna's name has been changed.

We also do patrols at noon, 4 p.m., and 8 p.m. These typically run through the Old City and out near the Ibrahimi Mosque and part of Shuhada Street, which runs alongside the back of CPT's apartment. During these patrols, we check the streets to see whether any harassment is occurring. If we observe any offenses, we dialogue with the Palestinian to learn his or her needs or wishes, document the incident through photographs and video, and in the case of violence, may get in between the agitator and the victim. Luckily, we have not seen any instances of violence. We hope things remain calm here.

We divide daily tasks at our apartment among the members of the team. We rotate the responsibilities of organizing morning worship, cooking dinner, and washing dishes. We will clean the apartment once per week, and we each have another designated role for the month, such as media coordinator, equipment supervisor, home manager, etc. We work well together, sitting around the table together each evening for dinner and often for lunch, discussing issues of occupation, strategies for peacemaking, and casual conversations for interpersonal relationship building.

My stay thus far has been insightful and beneficial, but exhausting and tense as well.

4

"Apartheid Street"

Monday, January 9, 2012—Hebron, Occupied Palestine

APARTHEID HAS PARTIALLY SUCCEEDED here. Shuhada Street is perhaps the best example of this success. Running parallel to the Old City, Shuhada Street (known to Hebronites as "Apartheid Street") was once one of Hebron's main thoroughfares, thriving from heavy foot and automobile traffic. In 2003, however, the IDF permanently closed this street to Palestinians, leaving it open only to settlers. Shuhada Street connects the settlements of Beit Romano, Beit Hadassah, and Tel Rumeida to the Old City and the settler-only Gutnick Center near the Ibrahimi Mosque. Our apartment overlooks Shuhada Street, and the small road running beside our front door intersects with Shuhada. This small road used to be one of the busiest in Hebron, full of markets and crowds. Now, a wall and barbed wire blocks the intersection, and our street is empty.

Tragically, this implementation of apartheid has forced many Palestinians living along Shuhada to vacate their homes because they cannot enter or exit without using the street, which is forbidden under penalty of arrest. Those who are able to remain in their homes must exit from the back of the house and then often travel much longer distances to get to very near locations. To get to Qeitun, one of the checkpoints we monitor in the mornings, from the Old City and the Mosque, one must cross Shuhada Street. The IDF has set up a road block along a small part of Shuhada so that the

Palestinians can walk *along* it without walking *on* it. After 40 or 50 yards, the road block ends, and a soldier dutifully watches as Palestinians briefly cross over Shuhada to reach houses and schools near Qeitun and beyond. The soldiers are stationed along this section of the road to "protect" the settlers who pass by. (I use quotation marks because the *vast* majority of violence between settlers and Palestinians is instigated and perpetuated by the settlers).

On Friday, after noon prayers, three young Palestinians boys, no more than four or five years old, were kicking a Coke bottle for fun, playing a makeshift soccer game. They kicked the bottle down the ramp-like passageway that runs from the Mosque to Shuhada Street, next to the Gutnick Center. Caught up in their game, they accidentally kicked the bottle under the roadblock, and it rolled onto the street. The bottle stopped next to a soldier, and they petitioned him to return it, arms outstretched to receive it. He looked down at them, shrugged, and then kicked the bottle away to another soldier. The boys ran over toward him, a cement barrier in between themselves and the soldier. He too shot them a glance and then kicked the bottle behind him to another soldier who then turned and punted it across the street, destroying all hope for the boys to get back their object of joy. Defeated, the boys dropped their heads as they prepared to move on.

Chris and I stood at a Palestinian man's shop, watching in dismay as the event unfolded. Even after all I have seen, read, and heard regarding Palestine, I was still shocked by the soldiers' arbitrary meanness to these little boys. Do they not realize that actions like these are what cause young Palestinian boys to grow up to hate Israelis? These actions perpetuate the cycle of hatred. Hoping to undermine these actions, I walked over to the dented plastic bottle, picked it up, and, standing next to the soldiers, handed the bottle over the barrier, returning it to the boys. Through big smiles they exclaimed, "*Shukran!* Thank you!" and ran off laughing. As I turned to walk back to Chris, I could feel the stares of the soldiers beating down on me. One of them glared at me for a few minutes, his expression one of disbelief. I suspect they did not appreciate me subverting their authority.

No action was taken by the soldiers toward me, however. I told Jean and Chris that I was sure I had now found my way onto the soldiers' blacklist. Yet, I have continued to patrol that area, even at night, and the soldiers have not even spoken to me. Hopefully, all will be well. Yet, I knew that I could not sufficiently or effectively do this job if I was not willing to take risk. I pray I choose my battles wisely. Much to my relief, the team affirmed my intervention. Perhaps next time, the soldiers will give the children back their bottle. *Inshallah*, God willing.

5

Amir's Arrest

Wednesday, January 11, 2012—Hebron, Occupied Palestine

MORNING SCHOOL PATROLS WERE quiet on Monday. Breakfast and worship were nourishing. The day felt normal, even when an IDF soldier told us he must check even the bags of school children at the checkpoint because "any of them could be a terrorist." And then Chris called. Soldiers were harassing a young Palestinian man in the Old City, close to our apartment. I gathered my things and ran out onto our empty street, heading toward the shops of the Old City.

I arrived on scene to find four soldiers in a semicircle, setting up a blockade, as two others had a young man pushed against the wall. Chris, who had witnessed the incident from the start, informed me that the young man, named Amir, was sitting in his chair when the soldiers seized him.[1] I promptly began filming them. The soldiers secured Amir's hands behind him with plastic ties and then began moving him through the Old City. Two soldiers lagged slightly behind, presumably to keep Chris and me from getting too close as we followed them. One of these soldiers appeared very agitated at our pursuit, glancing back at us often. His fellow soldier tried to keep him calm.

Chris called TIPH (Temporary International Presence in Hebron), as is protocol, but we had great difficulty describing our location because

1. Amir's name has been changed.

15

the soldiers had taken Amir down side streets, away from the familiar areas.[2] They eventually entered a large archway into an area that seemed to be nothing more than a dark cave beneath some houses. We wondered if they had taken him there to beat him, but it turned out to be a passageway leading to more alleyways and an entrance to the Avraham Avinu Israeli settlement, which sits right in the heart of the Old City, adjacent to and atop Palestinian homes and shops. The metal door to the settlement shut and locked behind the soldiers, and they disappeared around a barrier. We could see into the settlement via a small window in the door, through which we yelled to the soldiers, demanding an explanation for the arrest. We received no response.

Kathy soon arrived, having received our call, and she conveyed our whereabouts to TIPH, who informed us they were in transit and would call us upon their arrival. Kathy, Chris, and I tried to formulate a plan. Certainly we would wait there until Amir's release, but was there more we could do? Kathy expressed fear that the soldiers would release Amir onto Shuhada Street, leaving him vulnerable to the settlers. We decided I should go to Shuhada Street, pretending to be a tourist, and watch for his release.

I left Kathy and Chris and moved quickly back through the Old City toward the apartment. Once there, I removed my CPT hat and vest, grabbed my backpack, guidebook, and Chris's Cleveland Browns winter hat and headed for Shuhada. The soldiers at the Shuhada checkpoint stopped me, asked for my passport, and inquired as to the purpose for my trip to Hebron. Feigning ignorance of the political situation, and imitating the Southern accents of my home, I held up my Lonely Planet guidebook and said, "I don't know. It's in the guidebook. Thought I might check out the tomb of Abraham or something." The soldier holding my passport noticed my visa stamps from my summer visit of 2010. After asking me why I was back, I told him I had more to see.

"Oh, you love Israel?" the other soldier asked me, smiling. Before I could answer, the soldier with my passport interjected, "Do you love Israel or Palestine?" He was suspicious, something I had feared due to my presence at this checkpoint just a few hours before while on patrol. I had hoped the different hat, sunglasses, and backpack would be enough to throw them off. Apparently he needed more convincing.

2. TIPH has been present in Hebron for well over ten years now. They are officially recognized by both the Palestinian and Israeli governments and thus have more political clout and influence than other observer organizations. Officially, TIPH is neutral. They are there strictly as unbiased observers.

Pretending not to understand his distinction, I asked, "Well, where are we right now?"

"This is all Israel," he said. "All the land."

"Well, hell! I guess I love Israel!" I said. At this, they both appeared satisfied and, wishing me well, handed me my passport and sent me on my way. (Generally, I do not advocate amusing soldiers by telling them what they want to hear, but in this case, I needed to get down Shuhada Street without a hassle.) I walked down Shuhada, passed the Beit Hadassah settlement, passed the Beit Romano settlement, to Avraham Avinu. Kathy told me that TIPH and ISM (International Solidarity Movement) should already be there, but I saw no sign of them. While pretending to read my guidebook, I sat on the sidewalk outside the settlement, looking for any sign of Amir. After a while, it seemed clear that TIPH and ISM were not coming, and Kathy felt it wise I not stay there long as someone might recognize me as a CPTer. I agreed and headed back.

When I finally rejoined Kathy and Chris, the soldiers had been holding Amir for nearly two hours. Chris had managed to sustain a conversation with a soldier for some time, but was not having much luck getting information on Amir. The soldier finally walked away, and Chris decided to head back to the apartment to get his lunch that had now been delayed a couple of hours. Kathy and I sat in the dirt of that backstreet, talking and waiting. Occasionally, I rose and pounded on the door, asking where Amir was. I could see only one soldier, who stood about 30 yards from the door. I consistently received the same response from him: an apathetic shrug. After a few attempts, asking in English and Hebrew, I sat back down, uncomfortable with not knowing what was happening to Amir and frustrated that I was so powerless to help him.

Suddenly, I heard a commotion coming from inside the settlement. Rosie had just joined us, and the two of us moved quickly to the door. Peering through the window, I saw about six soldiers standing in a cluster. After a few seconds, they separated, revealing Amir, arms still bound behind him, sitting in a plastic chair, blindfolded. "What is that?" I yelled repeatedly, body nearly shaking in anger. The soldiers looked at me, waited a few moments, and then moved Amir back out of sight. I still am unsure if this act was to assure us Amir was not terribly injured, or rather to flaunt their power, reminding us that *they* had Amir, and we could do nothing about it.

I continued calling through the window to the soldiers, and finally one of them started toward me. "What do you want," he asked disdainfully.

"When will you release Amir?" I responded. He shrugged, flicked his head upwards (a sign of frustration), and waved his hand to dismiss me as he turned back.

The next fifteen minutes crawled by. Rosie, Kathy, and I tried to make conversation to pass the time, but we all felt tense. Finally, two soldiers walked toward the door with Amir between them, still blindfolded and bound. They stepped through the doorway, and one soldier began cutting off the plastic ties as the other removed the blindfold. Amir grimaced as the soldier cut the ties, a process that oddly took him a couple of minutes. Once they removed the blindfold, Amir nodded to us without smiling, acknowledging our attempt at solidarity. I filmed as Rosie confronted one of the soldiers.

"Why did you arrest him? What did he do?" she asked.

The soldier looked annoyed. "I have my reasons." His finger poised on the trigger of his gun.

"You have *your* reasons? It is a public act, though. It is an invasion of his rights," she protested.

"No, it's not."

"Yes it is," Kathy, Rosie, and I countered in unison. Rosie continued, "We just want to know why you did it. It's contrary to his rights."

"I don't have to tell you anything," the soldier responded.

Rosie argued that soldiers cannot arrest civilians; only police are permitted to do so. "No, soldiers too," he replied. Legally speaking, she was right. In practice, though, he was too. Soldiers here do as they wish.

"What's your name?" I asked the soldier, who dismissed the question. I persisted, "Why won't you tell me your name?" By this time, a third soldier had joined the others, and he said he would give me his name. "Bond," he said. "James Bond."

The soldier finally finished cutting the plastic ties from Amir's hands, and the soldier with whom we had been conversing now removed his finger from the trigger. The soldiers returned into the settlement, and we turned to walk with Amir back through the Old City. As the door closed behind the soldiers, I raised my voice, "You should be ashamed of this."

Amir showed us his hands, which were dried, purple, and swollen. I could clearly see the mark of the plastic ties deeply indented in his skin, evidence of excessive tightness. We walked with Amir back onto the main street of the Old City. He was immediately greeted by other young Palestinian men, who laughed and patted him on the back. The laughter confused me, until I learned that soldiers have arrested Amir around twenty times. Fatima, a good friend of CPT, told us that most of the *shebaab* have been arrested numerous times.[3] It almost seems to have become a joke among them: Who will be arrested next? The soldiers come up with various reasons to arrest the *shebaab*. Rarely do any of these excuses prove to be legitimate security concerns.

But what was Amir's crime *this* time? Why was he arrested while sitting in his chair, then blindfolded and bound tightly, and detained for two and a half hours in the cold? Simple: One of the soldiers did not like the way Amir looked at him. That was all it took.

3. Fatima's name has been changed.

6

The Struggles of the Past Week

Friday, January 13, 2012—Hebron, Occupied Palestine

THIS WEEK HAS BEEN intense. A new group of soldiers, called the Golani Brigade, arrived on Sunday. Perhaps these fresh legs are why tensions have grown. The soldiers' harassment of Palestinians worsened this week. It seemed each CPT patrol had an incident. On one patrol, Jean and I came across a group of eight Palestinian teenagers at a checkpoint. The soldiers had taken each of the boys IDs and had been detaining them for at least fifteen minutes already. One boy in particular paced in frustration because he was on his way to an important engagement. I stood talking with the boys, notebook and pen in hand, until one of the soldiers told me I must move back. "You cannot talk to them," he explained. I explained to him that I could. Again, he said, "No, you must move back. You can talk to them after. Not now."

"That makes no sense," I protested. "The conversation will be the same now as it will be later. Anyway, I can still talk to them from back there. Why do I have to move?" He gave me no reason. At Jean's request, though, I moved back, but also began filming the soldier so he would be sure I was still documenting the situation. After 20–25 minutes, the soldiers finally returned the IDs. At each of the next three checkpoints Jean and I visited that night, similar situations occurred.

As I was finishing a patrol with Chris recently, we approached the Mosque checkpoint which leads into the Old City, turning the corner in time to see one of the soldiers poised, weapon in hand, barrel resting on the wooden rail of his barricade, aiming down the walkway, readying his rifle. Palestinians walked back and forth in front of him, including a mother and child. Chris and I jumped forward. "What are you doing?" we exclaimed in disbelief. Another soldier burst out of the adjacent barricade, shouting at us, "It is not loaded! It is not loaded!"

"We didn't know that!" we protested. "You can't see the magazine the way he is holding the gun." Chris was filming, which made the soldier angry.

"You should ask me first! Now the world sees, and think soldiers are bad. Ask first!" We told the soldiers that the purpose of their act was to instill fear. "It is *not* loaded!" the soldier shouted again. "You should ask first! Ah! I fucking hate you!"

The harassment is not just from soldiers to Palestinians, though. Soldiers have also harassed CPT this week. We covered the patrols of EAPPI (Ecumenical Accompaniment Programme in Palestine and Israel) at Qurtuba School this week. Qurtuba School is off Shuhada Street, between the settlements of Tel Rumeida, Beit Hadassah, and Beit Romano. Settlers have been known to attack Palestinian children, and soldiers often harass Palestinians who walk from their homes to the checkpoints in this dangerous area. During our patrols, Chris received particular targeting from the soldiers. A group of six soldiers, the same group that arrested Amir, appear most responsible for the tension hanging over the city this week. Earlier this week, they arrested Amir. Yesterday, they beat and arrested two boys.[1] They patrol Shuhada Street, the Old City, and each of the checkpoints, looking for a reason to assert their authority and spread fear. A couple seem willing to talk when you ask them a question, but one of their leaders (the same one with whom we spoke when Amir was released) immediately hushes them and keeps their march moving. The soldiers have confronted us enough now that they all know Chris and me by name.

At least one attack by a settler has occurred against international observers. A stone whizzed by two young ISM women as they walked down Shuhada Street. Startled, they turned to see a settler woman running at them, "so angry she was shaking," as the ISMers reported. The settler punched the ISMers and then picked up a rock big enough that she needed

---

1. Story in next chapter.

two hands. At this, the two young women fled. Though Palestinians by far suffer the worst harassment and persecution, no one seems truly safe here.

The worst is still to come to be sure. Yesterday, the IDF destroyed the road blocks and the outpost at Al-Bweireh. (As a reminder, one of CPT's main tasks is escorting the children at Al-Bweireh who must walk long distances to reach their schools because the IDF had blocked the road so that no Palestinian cars could pass through. A long stretch of the road runs parallel to a settler road, which connects the settlement there to Outpost 26. Settlers have often attacked Palestinian children along this stretch of road.) The settlers are outraged that the military destroyed their outpost. The outpost (like all settler outposts), in theory and practice, was a means of expansion, but such outposts are illegal, even under Israeli law. To lose this outpost is devastating to them. In order to prevent retaliatory violence from the settlers, soldiers locked the gate of the settlement that opened onto the outpost road. The settlers then spent the whole day gathered in protest at the gate, even tearing it down at one point. The soldiers restored the gate and stood guard the remainder of the day and night. The nearby Shalhoub family house often suffers stone attacks from settlers.[2] After an event like the outpost destruction, "price-tag" attacks by settlers are normal. These can take place anywhere in the West Bank. The intent is to create such unrest that the military will not interfere in settler affairs again. All Hebron was tense yesterday.

At the family's request, Chris and I slept at the Shalhoub house last night, not only for solidarity with the family, but also to provide a feeling of security (particularly to the children), and to document any attack that happened, which thankfully, never occurred. Tensions will be high for the next few days, however. The locals believe a storm is coming. The weekly settler tour is on Saturday, and I do not know what to expect this time.[3] We pray all goes smoothly. A Jewish man told the team today that he expects the Israeli Supreme Court will mass approve scores of demolition plans for the outskirts of Hebron and the surrounding hills. The coming days could be disastrous.

2. The family's name has been changed.

3. Scheduled for every Saturday afternoon, the settler tour is an event when Jewish individuals and groups from Israel and elsewhere come to Hebron to receive a tour of the Old City from a popular settlement rabbi. Protected by dozens of heavily armed soldiers, the tour winds through the streets of the Old City as the rabbi tells the story of Jewish residence in Hebron, even indicating which houses Jews owned, and then recounts how a number of local Arabs massacred dozens of the Jewish inhabitants in 1929.

7

Assault

Saturday, January 14, 2012—Hebron, Occupied Palestine

ON THURSDAY EVENING, SOLDIERS forcibly entered a Palestinian family's home near the Qeitun checkpoint, assaulting the mother and two sons.[1] The invasion was a result of an earlier encounter between the soldiers and Halim, the older of the sons, eighteen years old and with developmental disabilities. In the morning, Halim was coming home through the Qeitun checkpoint after refilling the gas for the household. When he tried to enter the door of the checkpoint corridor, the soldiers closed it. He knocked repeatedly on the door until the soldiers shouted at him, "Why are you knocking?"

"Because you will not open the door to let me through," he responded. When the door opened and he exited the corridor, the soldiers knocked the gas can away, shoved him to the ground, and began beating him. When Halim tried to get up, he stumbled into one of the soldiers, who then claimed Halim attacked him. They took him into a side alley to continue the beating out of public sight.

A witness had called Halim's father, who arrived and took Halim home after a verbal confrontation with the soldiers. The soldiers did

1. With thanks to the family for recounting this story, and to CPT's neighbor Zleikha for the translation to English. The names of the young men in this story have been changed.

nothing during the day, though several Palestinians saw them lingering outside the family's home throughout the afternoon. Only a few minutes after TIPH passed by on evening patrol, the soldiers stopped Halim in front of his house. They said they had come for Nasser, Halim's sixteen-year-old brother, and would destroy the house if Halim did not retrieve Nasser. Halim called to his brother, who appeared at the front door up the stairs. Before he could descend, the soldiers bound up the stairs and grabbed him, dragging him outside, whereupon they handcuffed and blindfolded him and his brother. As they beat Halim, they pointed a gun to his head and threatened to kill him if he opened his mouth about what was happening.

The mother demanded to know why the soldiers were taking her boys, but the soldiers shoved her back and told her to "go home." They forced Nasser against the wall outside the house and began beating him with the butt of their rifles. He suffered frequent severe blows to the head. The members of the Israeli Defense Force then arrested Nasser and Halim, escorting them to the military base. During the march, Nasser began vomiting and then fainted from a concussion. Once at the military base, he fainted again.

The soldiers released Halim within the hour and transferred Nasser to the police station, evidently in an attempt to press charges. Due to the immediate action of the locals and international observer teams, the Red Cross, Hebron Rehabilitation Committee (HRC), Civil Administration (DCO), law offices, and other organizations soon got involved. The police released Nasser after a couple of hours, sending him home that night with a fractured skull, and additional injuries to the head, eye, hands, back, ribs, shoulders, and stomach. He was unable to sit when we arrived home because the pain was too overwhelming.

The soldiers have suffered no repercussions.

8

Rehumanization and the Danger of the Single Story

Tuesday, January 17, 2012—Hebron, Occupied Palestine

I RECENTLY HAD AN encounter with "the other." The stories I write involving soldiers sometimes portray them as almost inhuman. Witnessing the reality here, I often have difficulty seeing the soldiers as normal human beings, for in some ways, they have dehumanized themselves by their abhorrent actions against Palestinians. I write the stories the way I see and hear them. This results in soldiers appearing soulless at times, without decency or dignity. To hear of a soldier beating the head of a sixteen-year-old boy until his skull cracks and he vomits from a concussion causes me to doubt our common humanity. How is the soldier who abuses his power equally as human as the victim who suffers in nonviolence? The latter is asserting his or her humanity while the former is squelching it. I struggle to hide my looks of condemnation when I pass by the soldiers. Most of the time, loving—or moreover liking—an enemy who treats the innocent as subhuman feels impossible for me.

But this is the danger of the single story. Nigerian novelist Chimamanda Adichie warns of the danger of single stories—that is, stories which depict only one side to a person or event. Such stories, when repeated often, convince the audience that the description within the story is the whole truth. For example, right-wing American media preaches a single story of Arabs: They are terrorists. The only news they provide about the Arab world deals with Arab violence. The audience, therefore, is left believing that all Arabs are violent. Single stories, Adichie says, produce stereotypes. "The problem with stereotypes is not that they are untrue," she elaborates, "but rather that they are incomplete."[1] Arab people can be violent, like all other people, but violence does not define them.

I must confess, though, that I have a single story of soldiers. Not only soldiers really, but all those who abuse power and create suffering. I acknowledge that this single story is not my fault alone. Rather, the powerful often live a single story for the public. Before the eyes of the world, they can often act as tyrants. Their demonization is frequently their own doing. Yet, I want to take seriously Jesus's call to love my enemies, even (or perhaps especially) those who act like monsters. Without another story to add to the original, though, I cannot create a fabric of humanity in which to clothe them. I have needed a story to re-humanize the Israeli soldiers occupying this land. Ari gave me one.

I met Ari last week on morning patrol at Qurtuba School. He stood on one side of the street near the checkpoint, and I stood on the other side near the school stairs. For good or ill, I do not often initiate greetings or conversation with soldiers because many of the locals would not appreciate us seeming amicable with their occupiers. I did not greet Ari therefore when I arrived at the school early that morning. We exchanged looks and nods and went about our business.

His brown hat caught my eye first. The different groups of soldiers can be identified by the color of their hats. Border Police wear green hats (interesting that *Border Police* are in the middle of a Palestinian city in the West Bank, some distance from the Green Line border), paratroopers wear red, and Golani wear brown. Palestinians often regard the Golani Brigade as the real troublemakers. And, true to the stereotype, when Golani arrived in Hebron last Sunday, after several weeks of relative calm, the trouble began the next day.[2] Last week, Golani arrested Amir on Monday, increased ID checks, harassed Chris and myself numerous times, and beat Halim and Nasser on Thursday. This week, Golani members have continued harassing

1. Watch Adichie's TED talk at http://blog.ted.com/2009/10/07/the_danger_of_a/.

2. I later learned that the Golani Brigade actually arrived a few weeks earlier, in late December, and that Hebron was not as calm as I had originally thought.

young men and even invaded a home last night. They are troublemakers, and Ari is Golani.

After a few minutes of silence, he approached me. "Where are you from?" he asked, his tone unexpectedly friendly.

"The United States," I replied. "You?"

"Jerusalem," he smiled. He was proud of his hometown, and I wondered how many people throughout history had smiled that same way when claiming Jerusalem as their home. He continued the conversation, "How long are you here?"

"At Qurtuba or in Hebron?"

"Hebron," he clarified. I told him I was leaving in March but would still be in the country for another month. He told me he had been here since Sunday and would not be leaving for three months. His eyes looked away in resignation, and he stepped back. After looking up and down Shuhada Street, he returned to the conversation.

"Do you enjoy this job?" I asked as he approached.

He looked at me with confusion. "How could I enjoy this?"

I shrugged, "I have no idea, but some soldiers really seem to enjoy what they do."

He waved his hand around, motioning towards the settlements and Old City. "I signed up to protect Israel, not to do this shit."

Having drawn a distinction between national defense and the military presence in Hebron, he had now captured my full interest. "You don't want to be in the military?" I pursued.

"Who really *wants* that?" he asked, his English perfect. "I do want to protect Israel. But not this." He raised his eyebrows and looked up, which is a dismissive gesture here.

"You don't think this is protecting Israel?" I asked.

"I don't know," he shrugged. "Maybe . . . in some way. I don't know." I paused, wondering the right question to ask next. Before I could formulate it, he continued. "You must believe me, though, if the soldiers left Hebron, all the Jews [that is, the settlers] here would die."

"You think so?" I questioned.

"Of course," he nodded with confidence. "Also, if I went into Hebron without all this," motioning to his armor and weapon, "I would not come out again. Believe me."

"I am not so sure," I contested. "They do not all want to kill you. The only reason why it would be dangerous for you is because of the way soldiers treat people." After he asked for clarification, I told him about the Golani arresting Amir for looking at them with disrespect. He shook his head in disapproval. Almost all Palestinians I had met, I told him, do not inherently hate Jews or want to destroy Israel. They want to live in their land with the same rights as their Israeli Jewish neighbors.

"What about 1929?" Ari asked, referring to the 1929 Hebron Massacre, when Arabs tragically killed sixty-seven Jews here. Competing interpretations exist for the impetuses behind this massacre, some more viable than others. Whatever the reasons, however, many Arabs harbored Jews in their homes during this massacre, saving over four hundred. I wonder if Ari has heard that part of the story. Israeli settlers often use the 1929 Massacre as justification for returning to Hebron by any means necessary. They consider themselves "liberators."

"What about Deir Yassin? Or Baruch Goldstein?" I countered. Deir Yassin was a Palestinian village whose inhabitants were systematically murdered by Zionist forces and buried in a mass grave in April 1948, before the establishment of the State of Israel and its war of independence. The Zionist forces used this event to spread panic throughout the land, compelling thousands upon thousands of Palestinians to flee from their homes. The story of Baruch Goldstein took place in 1994, when Goldstein, an American Jewish physician, entered the Ibrahimi Mosque during morning prayer and opened fire on Muslim worshippers, killing twenty-nine and injuring one hundred and twenty-five. I continued, "My point is that everyone has a story, or stories, that they use to justify their hatred. But Jews and Arabs have lived in peace here for many years, especially before 1900. It was once Zionism came saying that a Jewish state had to be free of the indigenous Arabs that the problems really began. Most Palestinians don't mind Jews living in the land, as long as the Palestinians can live here too."

Ari did not respond, but looked pensive as he stepped away to check the ID of a Palestinian. A police car suddenly pulled up in front of me, and the officer opened the door. "Let me see your ID please." I knew police had the right to ask for our passports, but I still asked why he needed it. "We do this for all tourists."

"No you don't," I laughed, annoyed that he thought me so clueless. The officer instructed me to follow him, and he drove his car farther down the street. As I passed Ari, he expressed concern. "I don't know what's going on," I told him. "The officer told me to follow him."

Over the next several minutes, the officer asked me about my business in Hebron, how long I would be there, and why I was at the school. After answering the officer's questions, I looked back at Ari, who shook his head in confusion. I shrugged. Before the officer released me, he asked for my cell phone number. I told him I did not know it. He suggested I call *his* number and then he would have it. I agreed to this, thinking it strange that the officer would exchange numbers.

"What's your number?" I asked him. He paused.

"Never mind," he said, realizing the ramifications of giving out his number. He shut the door and drove away.

When I returned, Ari asked what happened. "He wanted my passport and phone number," I told him. "I don't know why." He shook his head in annoyance, and then resumed our earlier conversation.

"Look, I just want to protect the people," he said with genuine conviction.

"I can understand that," I replied, nodding. "But if a settler attacked a Palestinian, would you protect the Palestinian?"

"Yes," he said firmly.

"Really?"

"Really," he reaffirmed.

"I ask only because soldiers usually do nothing when settlers attack. A while back, a settler boy beat a Palestinian boy in the head with a rock. It happened near Machpelah [the Ibrahimi Mosque]. The soldiers on duty did nothing. They actually laughed." Ari shook his head in disapproval. "This is why Palestinians do not like soldiers." He nodded.

My patrol was now over. Before I left, I told him that I appreciated the way he treated people, asking them for their IDs politely, checking them quickly, and speaking to them in Arabic. During my patrol, Ari had asked each person how they were doing, apologized for having to check their IDs, and wished them a good day as they left. I told him that for as long as he was here he should continue treating people with respect. He agreed, and we parted ways.

Ari is twenty years old, speaks four languages, and has a hearty laugh. His mother is from the Netherlands and his father from Egypt. When he leaves the military, he wants to travel and is considering law school.

9

The Golani and the Struggle to be Peaceable

Sunday, January 22, 2012—Jerusalem[1]

OVERCOMING THE SINGLE STORY, refusing to grant it victory, is crucial in the struggle for reconciliation. Yet, while we seek to overcome the *single* story, we can still acknowledge the *predominant* one. In Hebron, there is no single story, but there *is* a predominant story, a normative story. Since the Golani Brigade arrived in Hebron, they have presented a predominant story. This is what they tell:

On Monday, January 9, Chris and I witnessed the Golani arrest Amir. They bound him with plastic ties, blindfolded him, hit his head, and held him for two and half hours for looking at them with "disrespect."

On Thursday, January 12, we received a report that the Golani beat Halim, a young developmentally disabled man, when he knocked on the checkpoint door after they closed it in front of him. That evening, they attacked his mother and severely beat Nasser, Halim's younger brother, cracking his skull, and then arrested the two brothers.

---

1. Though clearly Israel claims a unified Jerusalem as its capital, the status of the city has been contested at least back to the 1947 UN partition plan (Resolution 181). Talks of a Palestinian state insist that East Jerusalem will be their state's capital. In recognition of these contested claims, I have chosen not to designate Jerusalem by country, nor even by "East" or "West."

On Sunday, January 15, we received a report that the Golani sat in a jeep and watched as settlers torched the eighth car of a Palestinian family the previous night. That same night, the Golani entered another family's home at midnight, forcing the family outside in the cold. The Golani made the oldest son stand for two hours with his arms raised high against the wall. When they left, they told the family, "Next time look behind you. We will kick you out from the house, and we will take it."

On Monday, January 16, Kathy and I witnessed as Golani invaded a home in the Old City during night patrol because a single rock fell or was thrown on them from above. They were in full armor and wearing helmets.

On Tuesday, January 17, Rosie and I witnessed Golani patrolling through the busy Palestinian market in midday, disrupting the people as they shopped. The soldiers forced everyone to stand aside as they marched, randomly stopping two Palestinian men to check IDs. The younger man had to stand with his hands raised high on the wall for the six minutes it took to check his ID. They attempted to enter a family's home because they wanted to know why they allowed tourists on their roof. We later received a report from the father that the Golani returned to his home that night at 1 a.m. and pushed his family out of the house, including his eighteen-month-old son, and they hit the father in the head with a rifle, for which he received treatment at a hospital.

On Thursday, January 19, as I exited our stairwell door, six Golani soldiers arrived in front of it. (The door from the street opens to the stairwell. At the top of the first flight of stairs is a small patio, which has two doors, one to our apartment and one to our Palestinian neighbor's, Zleikha.) The soldier in front of the door radioed to headquarters for permission to enter. I spoke up, "This is my house. Why do you need to go in my house?" One of the soldiers looked at me smugly and replied, "Do you see all of these houses around you? They are all *my* house." With this, four soldiers entered the stairwell, and two remained on the street to block me from following the others. After twenty minutes, the four returned, along with Zleikha, who said the soldiers did not enter the CPT apartment, but went into hers instead, without a search warrant. They wanted to be sure her door, which opens onto Shuhada (or "Apartheid Street"), was secure, and they told her they would send someone to weld it shut soon. I followed them as they left and marched into a dark side alley, only to crawl through a hole in a decaying wall, entering a courtyard that was enclosed on all four sides by an eight-foot wall. The soldiers then turned and smiled at me, motioning for me to crawl through the hole and join them. I did not. Later that evening, Golani soldiers detained a member of ISM for "farting at a soldier." They called the police to arrest the international, and while the police did not press charges, they held the ISMer for a couple of hours. When the police released the volunteer at his apartment, the soldier in question told him, "I am going to be your worst nightmare."

On Friday, January 20, we received a report that Golani soldiers were holding a ten and twelve year-old boy behind the gate of the military base just outside the Old City. Kathy and I hustled to the scene, and I climbed on a large concrete block next to the gate in order to see over. The soldiers yelled at me to get down, but I was able to see the boys before I did. A witness said the boys had been covering their faces in the cold weather, but had not been throwing rocks as the soldiers claimed. The soldiers told the boys' parents they would release the boys if the parents brought them five other boys they wanted.

Being peaceable is difficult for me here. I seek to be true to that Way which calls me to love my enemies, pray for those who harm me, repay evil with good, and forgive not seven times, but rather seventy times seven. My struggle is not that I do not wish to be peaceable (though that is often difficult as well), but rather knowing how to be. Watching injustice happen daily before my eyes, I want to speak out, to verbally confront it. Yet, each day I become more convinced of the futility of such attempts. The soldiers do not listen to nor care what I say. My protests often seem only to cause more tension. I yearn to know how to be present here in a beneficial way.

I have often heard, "An enemy is someone whose story you do not yet know." I find great wisdom in these words. Yet, learning the other's story frequently seems impossible here. Storytelling requires a relational space, and this space does not exist while the powerful are active in their oppressions. Where is the space to learn the other's story in that context? Without the opportunity to participate in the disarming power of stories, how do we practice reconciliation here?

I believe the ultimate goal is always the establishment of beloved community, the creation of *shalom*, of wholeness and goodness. For beloved community to be realized, we cannot play a zero-sum game. One side cannot experience complete loss in order for the other to achieve total victory. Reconciliation cannot come about this way. Might perhaps the best way to help the Palestinians be to seek the softening of the soldiers' hearts? We aid the Palestinians by helping the soldiers, not in the practice of their oppressive actions but toward the realization of beloved community. Perhaps my role here (or at least part of my role) is to move the soldiers to capture a glimpse of the beloved community that is to come, to help them see the light of reconciliation, which at the moment flickers faintly.

The allure of heroism often tempts me, but I pray to resist such a pursuit. To seek to be a hero is to seek to have power. Power is so often the destroyer of relationships, the curse of peacemaking and *shalom*. My understanding of Christianity urges me to resist the achievement of power, and instead embrace powerlessness and weakness. I often do not know how to do this, but for now might it mean the acceptance of the fact that neither I nor CPT will bring peace here? We will not stop land confiscations or harassment. We will not get the settlers and soldiers to leave, nor compel the Israeli government to return all land occupied since 1967. We are indeed powerless. *I* am powerless. Perhaps then my task is simply *to be*, to be with the Palestinians in their suffering, standing and waiting in solidarity. Perhaps my task is to encourage the realization of reconciliation and beloved community by practicing it as best as I can, attempting to live out its reality. If I wait for the soldiers and settlers to initiate (or even join in) the pursuit of reconciliation, I may wait a long time. Perhaps my perspective should be, "No matter what they do, I am living reconciled." The apostle Paul said, "If it is possible, as far as it depends on you, live at peace with everyone" (Rom 12:18). Mahatma Gandhi continued the challenge: "Be the change you wish to see in the world." I wish it was as easy as it sounds.

10

The Powers of Destruction

Thursday, January 26, 2012—Hebron, Occupied Palestine

THEIR FACES LOOKED WORN, broken by despair. The mother's eyes, red from weeping, appeared distant. The youngest of the nine children cried aloud, tears running down her dirty cheeks, and the father shouted with exasperation to the heavens, calling on the name of Allah. Eight other children sat on the rubble of what used to be their home. Within minutes, Israel had created another homeless Palestinian family.

Yesterday, Chris, Rosie, and I arrived by taxi to Umm Al-Kheir, in the South Hebron Hills. The home already lay in shambles. In 2008, Israel had demolished this family's home, which sits adjacent to the settlement of Carmel. Because the family rebuilt their home on the same spot as the original, the demolition squad did not require a new demolition order to re-demolish the home.[1] A crowd gathered around the family, consoling and mourning. International teams—such as EAPPI, the UN, Operation Dove, and CPT—documented the ruin. The family's belongings lay in piles next to mounds of broken stone. My heart broke at the sight.

Home demolitions are one of the most devastating practices of the Israeli occupation. As Israel increases the construction of settler housing units in the West Bank, it also destroys Palestinian homes, continuing to

1. In my understanding, under Israeli law, if a demolished home is built thirty meters away from the original spot, a new demolition order must be issued.

displace the unwanted population. Often, Palestinians receive no explanation for the destruction of their homes. The military arrives, usually giving the family anywhere from ten minutes to one hour to vacate, and then the Caterpillar bulldozers begin their violence. Under Israeli law, Palestinians must obtain building permits from the Israeli government, yet these are rarely granted. Many Palestinians opt to build without the permit and risk demolition. After all, what other choice do they have under occupation?

We hitched a ride back to Hebron with our friend Hamed Qawasmeh, who works with the UN High Commissioner on Human Rights. Just outside Umm Al-Kheir, we stopped to investigate another commotion in the small village of Deirat. Several soldiers and many Palestinians stood in a cluster, engaged in a heated argument. Beside them, a home stood under construction. Much work remained before the home would be inhabitable. Moments before we arrived, the IDF had issued a stop-work order to the home's owners, demanding they cease all construction on the house. The IDF then confiscated all the family's construction tools and equipment.

We stood on the hill next to the house, watching the interaction taking place between the soldiers and the Palestinians on the muddy gravel road just thirty yards before us. An Israeli demolition worker attached his tractor to the family's trailer. After soldiers unsuccessfully tried to load the cement mixer onto the trailer, the tractor driver decided to come back for the mixer and began driving off with the trailer. He moved only fifteen yards before he came to an abrupt halt, and in the blink of an eye, dozens of Palestinians yelled out as they sprinted down the muddy road to the tractor. Soldiers were pushing Palestinians, and Palestinians were shoving back. Chris and I stood filming from the outside, and we spotted Rosie, camera in hand, standing right in the middle of the clashes. We had no idea what had happened. Then I saw his feet under the trailer.

I called over to Chris, "Someone is under the trailer! I can see his feet and can hear him shouting!" I bent down next to the trailer and saw a middle-aged Palestinian man, crying out in agony as he clutched his right leg, which lay motionless next to the large trailer wheel. This man owned the trailer the military was attempting to steal, and he had jumped underneath it to force the tractor driver to stop. But the driver did not stop until he had run over the man's leg, breaking it. Chris was now squatting next to me, and we both gazed at the man in disbelief. The hum of the tractor started again, and I looked up to see the driver back at the steering wheel, preparing to move forward.

"What is wrong with you?" I shouted at him. "There is a man underneath you!" Before I had time to formulate a plan, the tractor moved
forward. To my relief, however, the workers had disconnected the trailer,
so it sat still as the tractor trudged through the mud toward the main road.
Someone called the Palestinian Red Crescent (medical service), and soldiers attended to the man as they waited for the arrival of the ambulance.
They shooed away international photographers, ordering us farther and
farther back. The man screamed as they splinted his leg. He began gasping
and dry heaving, but then suddenly stopped, lying motionless and quiet on
the ground with eyes closed. I assumed he had gone unconscious from the
pain. We stayed until the ambulance arrived.

I sat in the back of the UN car as we drove the bumpy road back to
Hebron. My thoughts were scattered. Israel had arbitrarily destroyed the
home of a family with nine children, taken away their shelter from winter's bitter cold, and denied them their place of community and belonging.
Another family now faced the battle to continue building their home, and
without the necessary tools because Israel confiscated them without just
cause. But the resistance of the man who owned the trailer inspired me, to
throw oneself in front of the powers of destruction and shout, "You must
run me over in order to commit this offense!" I pray for that courage, for I
am terrified knowing that the tractor driver did not stop.[2]

---

2. Days later I learned that the Palestinian man was actually uninjured. He had faked
the injury, creating a scene to stop the confiscation of his property. Upon hearing this,
I could not help but admire his creative nonviolent resistance. Rather than attack the
soldiers stealing his property, he creates a scene, exposing the violence of their actions,
and successfully disabling them from confiscating his trailer at that time. Though my first
rendering of this part of the story turned out not to be fully factual (though I certainly
believed it to be at the time), I still consider it a "true story," as it exposes a truth about the
occupation. Had this man actually been run over, it would not have been the first such
case in Palestine. The story of Rachel Corrie quickly comes to mind, a twenty-three-year-
old American activist who was killed by an Israeli bulldozer as she stood between it and
a Palestinian home in Gaza.

11

Darkness Cannot Drive Out Darkness

Saturday, January 28, 2012—Hebron, Occupied Palestine

UNLIKE JERUSALEM, HEBRON'S OLD City has one main street.[1] It connects the Ibrahimi Mosque to Bab Al-Balideyya, an open square next to the Beit Romano settlement and military base. Along this cobblestone road, narrower streets branch off, meandering deeper into the Old City, intersecting with other less trafficked alleys. At night, the Old City is dark, with only the main road lit, and there only in scattered places. The side streets are often as black as the night.

Three nights ago, the CPT team was walking home in high spirits after celebrating our beloved Kathy's fiftieth birthday at one of our favorite local restaurants. As we entered the Old City, we glanced down the first side street on our left and noticed two soldiers standing in the darkness up against the wall, a few paces from the faint light of the main street. Both had their weapons in hand. Without much discussion, we decided to stay, hoping to be a de-escalating presence.

"Hi guys!" we greeted, voices raised. "How are you tonight?" The soldier in the front simply nodded. "What are you doing back here in the dark?" Chris continued. "Are you waiting for someone?"

---

1. A variation of this chapter appeared on CPT's website, February 7, 2012, (http://www.cpt.org/cptnet/2012/02/07/al-khalil-hebron-reflection-darkness-cannot -drive-out-darkness).

The soldier in front smiled, "We are waiting for the Messiah." Our laughter reverberated off the stone walls.

"You are waiting for the Messiah with guns?" I asked chuckling. The soldier shrugged, still smirking.

"Would you like some cake?" Kathy offered, presenting her chocolate birthday dessert. Rosie took off to retrieve forks from the house.

"Come on! I know you want some," I pursued, after they declined. "That smile on your face says it all." The soldier in front stifled his laughter.

Chris, Kathy, and I decided to maintain a casual presence, not forcing the soldiers into conversation but neither allowing their intimidating presence to dominate that space. Kathy handed me the cake and I posed for pictures with Markie, her stuffed rainbow unicorn (a tool of de-escalation). Over the next several minutes, we exchanged a few light-hearted remarks with the soldiers to keep tension minimal. Just as Rosie returned with forks, a group of female Oxford students on a stroll joined us, more than doubling our group. Our laughter and cheerful conversation penetrated the night's silence, bringing a smile to the faces of Palestinians walking by. Yet, as some of these individuals turned down the alley where the soldiers were hiding, many hesitated, a few even jumped back, at the sight of these armed men in the shadows.

Then, as we divided the cake among our group and loudly sang "Happy Birthday," the soldiers decided to leave, stepping out of the darkness and disappearing behind the gate of the military base.

I am reminded of the words of Martin Luther King, Jr. that decorate our living room wall: "Darkness cannot drive out darkness; only light can do that."

12

The Difficult Road Ahead

Saturday, February 4, 2012—Beit Sahour, Occupied Palestine

THE HALFWAY POINT. ONE month down, one to go. In some ways, this statement gives me energy; in other ways, it sucks the life out of me. The truth
is I am tired. I have that anxious feeling you get when the car tank is nearly
empty, and you are on edge knowing that at any moment the fuel will burn
out, the car will sputter to a halt, and you will be left stranded. Chris says
feeling burnt out after a month is normal. I do hope so because, otherwise,
I am not sure I am cut out for this type of peace work. I have not yet learned
how to sustain it. My deflated spirit gives me a new level of empathy (and
I use that word cautiously, knowing I can never truly empathize) for those
living under occupation. *I* am overwhelmed after *one* month, while having
the privileged opportunity to take "days off," not being the primary target of
Israeli aggression, and knowing I will soon leave here to return home. But
this *is* home to millions of Palestinians who cannot, but moreover, will not
leave. I search for energy from their *sumoud*, the Arabic word for steadfastness, the commitment to stay in your place no matter what.

The team is down to three now. Kathy left one week ago, and Rosie flew
out Monday. We are rising again at 6:30 as schools are back in session after a
two-week vacation. Patrols continue with at least three per day, more if we
receive calls that soldiers are out. We speak to groups that come through,
visit friends in and around Hebron, and try to maintain a house. Recently,

the team finished a lengthy report documenting Golani abuses over the past month. We also received documentation from ISM and EAPPI. This report was presented at a Protection Cluster meeting of the United Nations which met in Hebron last week. The UN is running with this report, hoping to get it published with Israeli and international media, all with the grand hope of removing the Golani, though I am not optimistic. We do hope, though, that neither the Palestinians nor the peacemaking and solidarity teams here will receive significant backlash once this document is released. But again, I am not optimistic.

In my experience, optimism is a rare treat in Palestine. I grow more and more convinced I will not see an end to the occupation in my lifetime, and less and less convinced that the Palestinians will ever get the independent state they so deeply desire. The occupation here is so complex and well-constructed. The masters of war and military puppeteers behind the scenes devise brilliant schemes to continue solidifying their control over the people and the land. I just attended a meeting in Jerusalem on Thursday about the creation of national parks in East Jerusalem. Israel is building national parks on Palestinian land to keep Palestinian villages from growing. There is no shortage of ideas for stealing Palestinian land.

Some of my disillusionment stems from the continued realization that CPT and other peacemaking teams here in Hebron are really not making a dent in the enormous machine that is the occupation. If I came back with CPT next year, the situation would be same. Yet, despite the shortcomings of international peacemaking, CPT is doing good work. We support the Palestinians in their resistance and irritate the Powers in their occupation. Recently, a soldier vented to me, "What are you doing here? You have no life. You come here only to make our jobs difficult. You are *always* getting in our way." I smiled at this, knowing she had just complimented CPT though she meant to discredit us. The knowledge that the soldiers are frustrated with us brings some satisfaction in that it means we are doing our work well. By one soldier's own admission, we are making their jobs more difficult. That encourages me.

So in the end, the reassuring and redeeming moments for me are found in visits with Hebronites in their shops in the Old City, restful trips here to Beit Sahour and Jerusalem, humanizing conversations with the occupiers, and remembering that, in the words of Archbishop Oscar Romero, we are "ministers, not messiahs." The Palestinians often say that all current efforts to end the occupation are being done for the next generation. Those living oppressed now will not see the fruits of their labor. As disheartening as this is, I continue to meditate on Romero's words, finding both encouragement and disillusionment. For now, I accept this paradox:

> We plant the seeds that one day will grow.
> We water the seeds already planted
> knowing that they hold future promise.
> We lay foundations that will need further development.
> We provide yeast that produces far beyond our capabilities.
> *We cannot do everything, and there is a sense of liberation*
> *in realizing that. This enables us to do something,*
> *and to do it very well.* It may be incomplete,
> but it is a beginning, a step along the way,
> an opportunity for the Lord's grace to enter and do the rest.
> We may never see the end results,
> but that is the difference between the master builder and the worker.
> We are workers, not master builders;
> ministers, not messiahs.
> We are prophets of a future not our own.
>
> —OSCAR ROMERO [1]

---

1. Quoted in Claiborne and Wilson-Hartgrove, *Becoming the Answer to Our Prayers*, 49, emphasis mine.

13

The Search for Human Interaction

Sunday, February 5, 2012—Hebron, Occupied Palestine

Legend holds that as St. Francis journeyed along the road searching for the meaning of God, he came upon a dead tree and in exasperation exclaimed, "Speak to me of God!" And behold, the tree began to bloom . . .

There is no formula for nonviolence. No "best approach" or "This is *guaranteed* to work." In my limited experience, much of nonviolent direct action is guesswork. Trial and error. Adaptation. A certain attempt at de-escalation might work beautifully today, but that same approach could fail miserably tomorrow. The practice of nonviolence seems to fail far more than it succeeds in bringing about immediate positive change. If we pursue nonviolence in the hopes of seeing instant results, we will often be left dissatisfied. For me, I aspire to practice nonviolence due to my firm convictions that this is both the call for all Christians, as well as the only true hope for the world. Our desire is for the establishment of *shalom, salaam,* peace, wholeness. We want beloved community. Will nonviolence get us there? I am not sure, but I know that violence never will and never can. Violence is destruction. How can it create wholeness and community?

All this to say, no one has a patent on nonviolent strategy. There are many approaches. Some on the CPT team feel that conversations with soldiers are unproductive, unhelpful, and perhaps even wrong. They say,

"These are the occupiers. Our job is not to be friends with them." I understand this perspective and respect the decisions of those who choose not to engage. For myself, though, I find the conversations necessary. To speak of practicing *nonviolence* is really too limiting. *Non-violence* is simply that: the lack of violence. While nonviolence is a crucial *aspect* of the pursuit of peace, the absence of violence is not the final goal. We seek to create a culture of life. The Powers of this world, the masters of war, plan strategies and tactics that perpetuate the cycles of destruction and further cement the culture of death that infects our earth. Within this darkness, we must create light. In the midst of this culture of death, we seek to embody a culture of life.

For now, this is why I pursue conversations with soldiers. These soldiers belong to the war machine, instruments of the puppeteers who orchestrate real-life tragedies. Left unengaged, they cast a dark shadow over the city. They are like wolves, prowling the streets day and night. They often present themselves as demons, monsters to be hated, and I know I have the capacity to hate them. When this happens, the culture of death wins. My task then is to do the hard work of rehumanization. For me, this cannot happen without personal interaction, *human* interaction. As I mentioned before, I do not believe you can truly "love your enemies" if you do not know them. Part of loving my enemies means I hold them accountable for their actions, try to speak truth to their injustice. It also means, if possible, that when the soldiers are not active in their harassment, I need to create the space for meaningful engagement. If they choose not to participate, so be it, but the space is still there.

In some small way, I see this as an attempt to practice resurrection, experiencing life where death once dwelled. Often, these moments are brief. Last week, I walked through the checkpoint outside the Ibrahimi Mosque and encountered the soldier who informed me that I had "no life" and was only there to make their jobs more difficult. Another soldier, whose name I learned later but will here call Yakov, turned to me and said with disdain, "CPT is garbage. *You* are garbage."

I smiled, tilting my head in curiosity. "Do you watch tennis?" I asked. Yakov hesitated and then nodded, pretending to swing a racquet.

"You look just like Novak Djokovic," I commented, referring to a famous professional tennis player from Serbia.

"Djokovic?" The few other soldiers around him began discussing in Hebrew, seemingly giving their perspectives on my observation. A smile crept onto Yakov's face, and he then spoke to me in Hebrew. I turned to the female soldier who had just told me I had "no life." Smiling, she translated, "He thinks *you* look like Djokovic."

"Me?" I protested. "No way. My beard is way too thick." At that moment, we all were smiling. All of us. Moments before, CPT and I were under verbal attack. But now, everyone was laughing and chatting about tennis.

Other times, these moments come in the form of sustained conversation. Such was the case with Ari, or more recently, Dov. Dov is one of the Border Police, stationed at the checkpoints near the Mosque and the Gutnick settler center. I stood on checkpoint-watch at the Mosque Wednesday morning when I heard Dov convincingly impersonating a British accent. I stepped forward to applaud and was subsequently asked to try the accent for myself. I received an enthusiastic ovation for my effort. Dov meandered over next to me, and we spent the next forty minutes discussing a range of subjects, covering favorite movies, family history, love lives, desired travel destinations, and favorite places in Israel. After laying this groundwork, I saw space to push forward.

"When do you leave the military?" I asked.

"One month," he grinned. "I'm excited. I hate this job. Hate everything about it."

Earlier, one of the soldiers had asked me if I enjoyed taking pictures of soldiers beating children. "Of course not," I told them. "I wish you wouldn't beat children." Dov responded by saying that soldiers should never beat children, but that children often cause problems for them. The children, he said, yell at the soldiers, cussing at them and spouting all kinds of vulgarity. He told me he feels he should sternly reprimand but never beat them. In light of his statement about hating his job, I felt now was a good time to follow up the earlier conversation.

"So you don't think soldiers should beat people?"

"No, of course not," Dov insisted, his body hunched over as he leaned against the railing. "Only an eye for an eye, you know. This is it. Do you know of this?"

"Sure I know of this," I assured. "It's part of my scriptures as well. But Christians also follow the teachings of Yeshua, and he went even further, telling us to love our enemies."

"Love your enemies, huh?" Dov asked, smiling.

"Yeah, kind of sucks, doesn't it?" We both laughed, as I continued, "But that's one reason why we are committed to nonviolence. You know, even if someone attacks us, we try not to fight back."

Dov looked up at me, "I want to be this kind of person."

"Hard to do with a gun," I said, pointing to the M-16 strapped to his side.

"I never use it," he replied.

I told him he should get rid of all his guns when he leaves the military. He nodded, "There is no need for them."

Exchanges such as these are helpful. Like a flash mob, these human moments appear and captivate, and then, just as quickly, vanish as if they never existed. But you leave knowing that they did exist, even if only for a moment. During those forty minutes, I tried to engage Dov not as an oppressor, but as another twenty-two-year-old man searching through questions, unsure of purpose or direction.

Such interactions are rare, however. Most of the time, the soldiers ignore me at best and threaten me at worst. They cuss, yell, and spit at me. *This* is normative. And despite those glimpses into the culture of life, in the end, Dov, Ari, and Yakov are still taking part in a brutal oppression. They are humans participating in the theft of other humans' land and resources.

Thus, should the search then not be for *human* interactions, but rather to rescue ourselves from the *devastation* of our own humanity? I wonder if the real problem is that our humanity is dying, choked by the myths and hatred we grasp so tightly. Like St. Francis, I keep shouting to this dying tree, "Speak to me of God!" But how long will we wait until the blossoms come?

Lord, have mercy. Christ, have mercy.

14

Home Invasions

Wednesday, February 8, 2012—Hebron, Occupied Palestine

ONCE AGAIN, EVENTS SUCH as these make it difficult to love my enemies.

Early this morning, over twenty Israeli soldiers raided and ransacked around forty houses in Hebron's Old City. Soldiers tore through the city, breaking down doors, searching houses, tossing rooms, and physically and verbally harassing the inhabitants who were asleep before the soldiers entered. Soldiers also broke down the door of the Ministry of Labor, which was empty in the early morning hours.

Chris, Carrie (our new teammate),[1] and I visited a family whose home the Border Police invaded around 1:30 a.m., awakening everyone. The soldiers wrote down the names and ID numbers of all eight family members, including two children, before leaving. Then, shortly before 4:00 a.m., twelve soldiers from the Golani Brigade forced their way into the house and ordered the family, including the two small children, into one room. The soldiers ransacked the rest of the home, breaking the locks on interior doors and tossing belongings onto the floor. They remained in the house until almost 7:00 a.m., not allowing the family to use the restroom. The family told us that the soldiers stole money and a child's wristwatch during the raid.

---

1. Carrie's name has been changed.

Another family showed us their house, the frame bent and the door dented from the soldiers' pounding. Several door handles must be replaced due to forcible entry with pry-bars. Boot prints were still visible on doors, and belongings remained scattered about bedrooms.

Another organization spoke with a family whose toddler daughter has significant trouble breathing due to severe developmental disabilities. Soldiers locked the child in a room alone and forced the family to wait outside in the cold while the soldiers searched the house.

In another case, soldiers forced two women who were alone with five children into the street for four hours while they broke all the doors of the house. One man reported that soldiers entered into his home, claiming that his children, both under the age of four, had been throwing rocks. Soldiers invaded another home, also accusing a man's children of throwing stones, whereupon the man informed them that he in fact had no children.

Local radio broadcast indicates that such invasions took place in at least two other West Bank cities at the same time, perhaps evident of a larger military operation. Locals have asked us to patrol the Old City after midnight as they expect the soldiers to return in the early hours. Chris has gone to Jerusalem on his day off, so Carrie and I remain here alone. Anxiety is beginning to set in.

15

I Hate Occupation

Wednesday, February 15, 2012—Hebron, Occupied Palestine

I HATE OCCUPATION. AT times, I almost feel I can physically smell the stench of the rotten mess of this systemic oppression. This morning, the team sat together for meeting and check-ins, a time when we convey to each other "where we are." At Carrie's suggestion, we also shared a wish-list of situations or events we wish could occur, even if we know it is impossible. During noon patrol, I reflected more on my wish-list and noticed that the wish residing at the core of all my emotions is this: to be able to visit Palestine when the occupation is no more. I know this sounds simple, romantic, even obvious, but it is a profound feeling for me, especially due to my current belief that I will never see the end of this occupation. In some ways, I have despised this city since my arrival. It drains me of energy, makes me want to stay in bed in the morning and go to sleep early at night to escape its sadness. It is certainly one of my least favorite places of all my travels. Yet, as I walked this afternoon, I realized the place has nothing to do with these emotions. Hebron's *beautiful* portrait has been smeared and splattered with checkpoints, roadblocks, settlements, settlers, and soldiers. The occupation is killing Hebron, and its people are suffering.

Yet, they resist. Through life, they resist. By opening their shops in the Old City day after day, they resist. By refusing to close their shops during settler tours, they resist. By continuing to shop in the market while soldiers patrol the streets, they resist. By denying the checkpoints or settler violence the power to hinder their children's education, they resist. By building homes when Israel threatens demolition at any moment, they resist. By planting crops season after season though settlers often steal the produce or burn the fields, they resist. By refusing offers of millions of dollars to sell their homes to settlers, they resist. By taking harassment and beatings from soldiers at a checkpoint one day and revisiting that same checkpoint the next, they resist. By returning to their roofs to work when just hours before settlers stoned them for doing so, they resist. In short, they resist through living life. Oh how I wish for these old farmers, hands stained from the soil they work, to have *one* season when they could nurture their fields in peace, experiencing the joy of liberation! I say again, I hate occupation.

This past week was full of activities, some intense, some relaxing. On Sunday, Carrie and I joined dozens of women and men in a protest for the rights of Palestinian prisoners being held in administrative detention within Israel. Israel uses administrative detention to imprison Palestinians indefinitely without charge, simply citing them as "security threats." Israel continues to hold Palestinian men imprisoned as far back as the 1970s, still no charge, still no trial. This is the Israeli version of Guantanamo Bay. As some may know, Khader Adnan is over sixty days into a hunger strike after entering administrative detention. Doctors say he is close to death. This week, Israel denied his appeal. But the hunger strike continues.[1]

The Hebron Governorate held a press conference Sunday for the release of the report CPT and other organizations have compiled on the Golani abuses since their arrival in late December. *Ha'aretz*, the main Israeli news source, has already run a story on the report, and more and more news organizations are picking it up each day. Due to the nature of the report, we wondered if we would experience any consequences from the Golani after releasing it to the public. Judging by the last few days, I think we will.

---

1. Adnan ended his hunger strike at sixty-six days in exchange for an agreement with Israel to be released mid-April 2012. This fast sparked a massive nonviolent resistance movement among Palestinian political prisoners, resulting in nearly two thousand prisoners of Israeli administrative detention participating in the largest hunger strike in known history beginning in April and ending in mid-May 2012. Gazan soccer player Mahmoud al-Sarsak took his hunger strike the furthest, refusing food for over ninety days in protest of his three-year imprisonment. Israel released him back into Gaza in July 2012.

Tuesday evening, responding to a phone call from a local shop owner, Chris and I arrived on scene to find six Golani soldiers frisking three Palestinian men in the Old City. Immediately, the leader of the squad approached me. I recognized him as the soldier who always calls himself James Bond when I ask his name. Several weeks earlier, Kathy and I followed his squad on a patrol at nightfall through the Old City. In an attempt to de-escalate, we began singing traditional hymns and freedom songs. When the patrol paused outside a home for a few minutes, I mustered up the courage to sing out solo, letting R. Kelly's "I Believe I Can Fly" ring through the still air. The soldier identifying as James Bond smiled, and then joined in. Soon after, two other soldiers added their voices to our a cappella chorus. Apparently we established a connection that night because he approached me Tuesday, hand extended, and greeted me, "Hello, my friend."

He informed me that Chris and I needed to stand ten meters back so as not to get in their way. Knowing we had little choice, we agreed and moved away, Chris filming all the while. We followed as the patrol moved on and then randomly stopped another Palestinian young man, frisking him against the wall. Bond motioned for me to come.

"You cannot follow us," he now said. "We are doing our job."

"Ok," I replied. "You have to search people because it's your job. We follow you because it's ours."

He wagged his large finger in front of my face, shaking his head. "You are Johnny," (not sure why he calls me that), "I am Bond. We respect you, and we don't want any problems. But if you keep following us, we will have to arrest you. This is a new law."

I grinned at him suspiciously, "So if I call my lawyer *right now* and he tells me that no such law exists, then we can follow you, yeah?" He smiled and nodded in agreement, reaching out his hand again to confirm the compromise.

Calling the lawyer, I learned that indeed no such law existed. The only law regarding this entails that internationals cannot "interfere" with soldiers doing policing. The catch? Soldiers decide what constitutes "interfering." Chris and I continued following from a good distance, still filming as the soldiers stopped another man to search. Upon seeing us, they motioned to me again and asked, "What are you still doing here?"

"I called the lawyer," I said, "and he told me there is no law that says we cannot follow, as long as we don't interfere."

"No, you cannot follow," Bond replied firmly.

"Ah, but you *just* said that if the lawyer said we could, then we could," I reminded.

"No, you cannot."

"But, you said . . . "

"*I* am the lawyer, ok?" he interrupted, raising his voice and pounding his fingers against his chest. "I am the lawyer."

The soldiers then instructed me that Chris and I had one more chance. They would leave us here, and if we followed again, they would arrest us. The squad then stopped a young Palestinian boy and escorted him down the street, out of our view. Chris and I are confident the soldiers used the child as bait to lure us into following them. Fortunately, they released the boy within a few minutes, and then returned inside the gates of their base.

This event is part of a series of recent attempts by soldiers to prohibit us, ISM, and EAPPI from documenting, refusing to allow us to film soldiers or checkpoints, prohibiting us from documenting the safe passage of school children at checkpoints in the morning, and now forbidding us from following patrols. Chris, Carrie, and I dialogue continually about how to continue our work in the coming days. We want to avoid arrest as that could potentially lead to deportation and hinder any future visits, but the work must continue. Much discernment ahead.

Other recent events include a soldier pointing his gun directly in my face from two feet away as he turned a corner in the Old City during a military drill; a hysterical settler woman slapping the face of a Palestinian police officer who was escorting the Deputy Prime Minster of Sweden down Shuhada Street, where apartheid forbids the passage of Palestinians; and the Gutnick settler center changing the name of their public wireless internet from "deathtopalestine" to "Kill Issa Amro," the name of a well-known Palestinian human rights activist here in Hebron.

I say again, I hate occupation. I hate *this* occupation. I mourn the fact I am powerless to end it. Through prayer and meditation, I continue to seek wisdom regarding the nature of my role here and the most supportive way to be in solidarity with the Palestinian people. This is a question I suspect I will ponder for years to come.

After Miriam, an eighteen-year-old Border Police soldier, asked me why I do this job for free, I told her, "I believe it's good work. I want to support suffering people."

"You want to help the Palestinians," she stated. I confirmed, and then there was silence.

"I don't hate Israelis, you know?" I smiled assuredly.

"No, no. You hate occupation." She paused, her eyes distant, as if deep in reflection. "I get that."

16

Open Shuhada Street

Thursday, February 23, 2012—Hebron, Occupied Palestine

It's OPEN SHUHADA STREET week. Issa Amro, human rights activist and director of Youth Against Settlements, has organized demonstrations and activities for each day of the week, building up to major actions on Friday and Saturday, the anniversary of the Baruch Goldstein massacre of 1994. This week represents the outcry of the Hebron people, the broader Palestinian population, and international supporters for an end to apartheid, an end to systemic discrimination, racism, and ethnic cleansing. Sunday was the opening of the week of the demonstrations, which began with a visit from Palestinian Israeli Knesset member Haneen Zo'abi.

Haneen's walk with Issa up Shuhada Street was met with shouts from angry settlers calling her a traitor and a terrorist, telling her the sea waited to swallow her, and ridiculing her for never marrying. To Issa they shouted insults like, "Each Arab dog shall have his day," and voiced death threats, consistent with the public announcement of the settler center's wireless internet network, "Kill Issa Amro." Tensions were high, especially when soldiers suddenly stopped all internationals and Palestinians from accompanying Issa and Haneen. The soldiers allowed a host of settlers through their barricade, but continued barring all other protective presence personnel. Helpless to do otherwise, we watched as settlers, shouting and waving Israeli flags, surrounded Issa and Haneen as they walked down Shuhada

Street. The soldiers gave us no explanation as to why they allowed settlers to pass but restricted our movement. Instead, they met our inquiries with harder and harder shoves, ordering us "Back! Back!" Issa and Haneen managed to break away from the settlers and take refuge in the Youth Against Settlements office on the hill.

After two days off in Beit Sahour, I arrived back in Hebron yesterday morning to hear that soldiers and police would be evicting a settler family that day. They had moved into the home of a Palestinian family who had no choice but to temporarily evacuate their home when Israel closed Shuhada Street to Palestinians. The Palestinian family never renounced ownership of the house, however. After months and months of running circles in Israeli courts, the family finally achieved a victory when the court issued the eviction order. The family asked for as many internationals and cameras as possible. The eviction of settlers is often violent, complete with fistfights and automatic weapons. As much as is possible, I prepared myself for chaos.

Numerous Palestinians, press, and a group of around twenty internationals (mostly from CPT, ISM, and EAPPI) joined the Palestinian owners of the house outside their stolen home on "Apartheid Street." The Israeli lawyer working on the case arrived and delivered the eviction notice, alongside military personnel, to the settler family. Those of us on the street were under close scrutiny from the numerous Golani and police present. The soldiers forced everyone to stand on the essentially nonexistent sidewalk, not one foot could be on the street. After twenty minutes, a police officer came around and collected each of our passports, effectively detaining us for as long as they saw fit.

Though they had just informed us that "taking photos is very rude," the soldiers and police began filming and photographing each of us. We all turned our backs to them to hide our faces, but they simply reached around our bodies, placing the cameras inches from our faces. One ISMer, who soldiers had arrested before, covered his face with a *keffiyeh* and refused the picture. After several failed attempts, a Golani captain made him move away from the group, isolating him from our protective shield. The soldier then made the ISMer (who took the pseudonym Aaron while in Hebron) remove everything from his bag and take off his jacket. Once Aaron had finished repacking his bag, a police officer walked over and began shoving several of us back, offering no explanation whatsoever. He then escorted Aaron to the other side of the street and put him through the same drill as the soldier—that is, "empty the bag and remove the jacket." After fifteen minutes, the officer informed Aaron they were taking him to the police station but refused to give any further explanation, simply saying, "I can take you where I wish."

In the end, the eviction never took place. The order was delivered but no additional action occurred. The police released Aaron two and a half hours after arresting him, and we all received our passports back an hour after the police had confiscated them and written down all our information. The soldiers escorted us through Checkpoint 56 and off Shuhada Street.

Tomorrow is the big showdown, the major action of the week. Organizers expect around two thousand people to show up tomorrow morning to "knock on the door of Shuhada Street." En masse, these protesters will attempt to enter Shuhada Street, refusing to accept apartheid's laws. Last year, the IDF fired tear gas, sound bombs, and rubber bullets at the 1,500 marching resisters. Organizers anticipate a similar response this year. CPT's assignment is documentation. We will try to film and photograph everything that happens. In the spirit of transparency, I confess that the anticipation of tomorrow's events churns my stomach. I am disquieted. But apartheid cannot be accepted.

As Issa announced Sunday night, "We cannot coexist with occupation."

17

The Action

Sunday, February 26, 2012—Hebron, Occupied Palestine

WHEN I AWOKE FRIDAY morning, all was quiet. After a simple breakfast and coffee, Chris, Carrie, and I walked through the Old City toward the Ibrahimi Mosque, heading to our friend Abed's shop near the settler center. The cobblestone streets were busy with people visiting the mosque in remembrance of the victims of the Goldstein massacre, which occurred eighteen years ago yesterday. The soldiers on duty did not seem unusually tense, despite the knowledge of the protest soon to come. My demeanor surely appeared similar, relaxed and unworried. In actuality, I struggled to sit still. My nerves compelled me to move.

Around 10:00, we walked through the Qeitun checkpoint and out of the Israeli-controlled area of Hebron. We arrived over an hour early to the demonstration's meeting place, a mosque a little more than a mile from the checkpoint. Our early arrival worked in our favor as a family across the street hustled out to greet us, bringing chairs, tea, homemade bread, falafel, and humus with olive oil made from the ancient trees in their backyard. Since no one in the family spoke English, the father sent for his neighbor's English-speaking son (who was asleep at the time) so that we would have a host who could talk with us. The young man awoke and came immediately. Hospitality is an art here.

The protesters began arriving close to 11:30, and by 12:15, around one thousand people stood on the street, holding signs and banners calling for end to apartheid and the reopening of Shuhada Street. As a team, our hope was to stay together, but we knew, once the chaos set in, that goal would be difficult to achieve. The march toward the checkpoint began with chants and waving flags. The energy was electric, pulsing through the crowd like the steady drumbeat that pounded through the air. *Keffiyehs*, traditional symbols of Palestinian nationalism and solidarity, hung around the necks of hundreds of people. Palestinians, Israelis, and internationals from all over the world stood side by side, joining together in this demonstration against the occupation and apartheid.

Filming and photographing, we walked along beside the mass of people, passed houses and shops full of Palestinians waving in support. Many people stood atop their roofs to see what would unfold. After a mile or so, we crossed over a three-way intersection and round a curve. Now we could see them. Sixty yards ahead of us, several heavily armored jeeps, numerous soldiers on foot, and a tank made an impenetrable wall across the street. Chris, Carrie, and I stood near the middle of the demonstration but in clear view of the front lines. Up ahead, I saw a single rock fly out from the crowd toward the armored brigade before us. The tear gas came within seconds.

Two loud shots rang out and the canisters sailed into the crowd, emitting a thick cloud of gas. Like a panicking stampede, people sprinted away, turning up alleyways and into houses and shops. The three of us ran up an incline off the main road to escape the gas, but it had already reached us. My nose and throat burned as if a fire raged inside. I could not stop coughing. Reaching for my camera bag, I frantically pulled out my bag of onions and put one to my nose and mouth and breathed through it. The steady coughing began to die down, but the burning remained. I knew of no other remedy for the pain than endurance.

We jogged across the street to the corner of the three-way intersection we had crossed earlier. From there, we could see the military position. A large group of *shebaab* formed the front lines of resistance, launching a barrage of stones at the army some thirty yards in front of them. With each volley of rocks came a counter volley of tear gas. The canisters sped out from the barrel of the tank, hitting both the front lines as well as the intersection where we stood. The crowds dispersed in an instant, everyone covering their faces with *keffiyehs* and onions. After several minutes, the people rejoined, ready to repeat the emerging pattern.

Over the next two hours, this cycle continued. *Shebaab* hurled rocks, and the army fired tear gas. In the ensuing chaos, I became separated from Chris and Carrie and found myself alone at the intersection, filming the lopsided battle. Everyone around me held onions in their hands, quick to offer pieces to anyone in need. Explosions pounded the air as the army launched sound bombs. Though these weapons produced no shrapnel, they were disorienting and terrifying. I saw tear gas canisters catapulted over the streets onto houses of uninvolved Palestinians, some with their children on the roof. Military jeeps would speed by as dozens of stones pelted their armor. Occasionally, these jeeps would swerve unexpectedly around a corner and soldiers would jump out throwing tear gas grenades and firing rubber bullets. I have never felt more fear than in those moments when the soldiers shot at us from their U.S.-made rifles. With tear gas burning my eyes like flames, I sprinted down alleyways, jumping over walls to take cover. Ambulances raced up and down the streets, picking up those injured from the tear gas and rubber bullets. Sirens whaled, sound bombs exploded, and tear gas blanketed the streets. I felt as if I was in a war zone.

Chris and Carrie filmed from a rooftop down the street, and I continued capturing footage from the intersection. The tit-for-tat attacks seemed endless. Rocks bounced off the solid frames of the military vehicles, and tear gas indiscriminately choked all who stood by. Full of adrenaline, *shebaab* would often rush to fresh tear gas canisters, pick them up while they still smoked, and hurl them back toward the military. Soldiers snuck through side streets, blindsiding the *shebaab* and trying to hit them with their rifles. While the tanks arched the tear gas into the crowd, these foot soldiers fired hand-held launchers directly at people. Like a rocket, one canister smashed into a wall only twenty feet to my right. As I backed away, another landed at my feet, and a large plume of gas leapt up into my face. My *keffiyeh* covered my mouth, but my eyes were exposed. The burning pain was some of the most intense I have yet felt. The gas managed to penetrate the *keffiyeh*, causing me to hack until I was sure I would cough blood. Chris and Carrie found me, doubled over against a wall, trying to breathe. A small Palestinian boy told me to sniff his cheap perfume. To my amazement, the coughing stopped, and after several minutes, the pain in my eyes faded.

Two hours after the chaos began, Chris, Carrie, and I decided to leave. No end was in sight, and we had captured more than enough footage. The crowd had shrunk to no more than a hundred *shebaab*. Our continued presence was unnecessary. A horrid stench greeted us as we walked back into the Old City. The military had showered the houses with Skunk, a chemical spray that smells like it sounds. I heard that the smell lingers on clothes for years and does not easily wash off skin. The city smelled of chemical waste. As I said before, the occupation reeks.

Allow me to share a brief reflection on the demonstration. After all was finished, I found myself asking the question, "What was the point?" As far as making changes, the action accomplished nothing. It did not stop the occupation. It did not open Shuhada Street, as we did not even *reach* it! However, I do not think this was the intent. The organizers and the participators knew nothing would change. They knew the army would stop the action with violence. There was no hope of victory. Rocks vs. tanks and semi-automatic weapons? The disparity is almost laughable. But change was not the point. The point was resistance. The point was to remind Israel that the Palestinian people are still here. They have not left, and they do not accept the systems of occupation and apartheid suffocating their existence. While one could certainly judge the rocks as unhelpful, they fly as tangible symbols of the spirit of resistance. Did this march change anything? Did it lift even part of the burden of oppression? No. But after one spends some time in here in Hebron, one cannot help but ask, "What else can they do?"

18

The Weekend

Monday, February 27, 2012—Hebron, Occupied Palestine

THE TENSION DID NOT end Friday. Consistent with their history over the last two months, the Golani continued their daily harassment of the people. Due to Friday's action, we expected Saturday's settler tour would be more problematic than usual. Everyone was on edge—the Palestinians, the soldiers, the settlers, and us. Additionally, Saturday marked the eighteenth anniversary of the Baruch Goldstein massacre. The tour had the potential to be toxic.

It occurred as usual, however. The settlers, guarded by more than thirty soldiers, toured the streets with no interference, while Palestinian mobility suffered under the constricting power of arbitrary military orders. When Palestinian *shebaab* dared to walk on their streets after the soldiers ordered them to wait to the side, soldiers moved the young men out of the way, taking close-up pictures of the their faces. At one point during the tour, as I stood clustered together with three other internationals, a soldier lifted his rifle, aiming it directly at us, and said, "I want to shoot you through the head with this bullet."

During the tour, the soldiers created a new rule. In the past, and even at the beginning of this particular tour, the soldiers instructed us to remain five meters away or they would arrest us. As the tour progressed, though, the rule changed. "You must be fifteen meters back or I will arrest you," the captain now ordered. This new rule conveniently disempowered us. In the ever-winding curves of the Old City, maintaining a fifteen-meter distance blocked our visual of the front line of soldiers, making documentation impossible. Only in select spots could we stand fifteen meters away and still see the soldiers. In these places, however, the soldiers would walk quickly in our direction, closing the distance between us, and would then observe, "You are not fifteen meters. Go or we will arrest you!" At one point, as the soldiers were detaining a journalist for photographing, the captain looked up at me, "You. Come here also." Backing away, I showed my open palms, explaining that I did not have a camera. He let me go.

On Sunday, Carrie and I returned from our trip to Al-Bweireh. She walked on to the apartment, while I stopped to buy eggs. As I made the hike back toward the Old City, I encountered a Golani patrol marching away from the military base toward Bab Al-Zawiye. Despite carrying two cartons of eggs, I decided to follow, careful to maintain a safe distance since I was alone. The soldiers turned off the main road and headed up amongst the houses. When the soldier in the back saw me, he greeted me with his middle finger raised high.

The soldiers stopped four young boys, no older than twelve. I saw the captain show the young boys pictures he took of the *shebaab* during the settler tour. He wanted the boys to help the soldiers find where these young men lived. I was dismayed at the predicament this captain put these children in: either disobey the armed soldiers or turn in your countrymen. The children led the soldiers away from the Old City, stopping at an intersection for some time. After ten minutes, two of the soldiers turned to me, shouting, "You cannot follow us! You know the law. You must go!"

"There is no law that says I can't follow you," I replied firmly but cautiously.

"You *know* the law," they repeated. "You are a lawbreaker." Biting my tongue, I decided it prudent not to enter into a discussion regarding who was the true lawbreaker. They alerted their captain, and he stepped forward, matter-of-factly telling me if I did not leave immediately, he would arrest me. Being alone, I could not risk this. Forced to leave, I zigzagged down the street slowly so as to prolong my visual of them. Eventually, I encountered Carrie, who had been trying to find me.

We returned to the Old City and visited our friend Fatima in her shop. After several minutes, word came that settlers were on a Palestinian family's roof in the Old City, just down the street. We hustled to the doorway of the home and ran up the stairs. The house is directly across from the Avriham Avinu settlement in the center of the Old City. The Palestinian family had received a work permit to fix the roof of their home, applying cement to patch up holes through which water was leaking into the house. The settlers, upset that Palestinians were permitted to repair their own home, crossed over the rooftops, invading the family's roof space, stepping in the wet cement, and harassing the family at work. A few weeks before, settlers had thrown stones and broken boards at the family as they repaired the roof. This time, they felt obliged to pay a personal visit. The distance between the home and the settlement is no more than twenty feet.

When we reached the top, I immediately saw the Golani squad I had followed earlier. They had come to intervene. The moment the captain saw me he ordered me to leave or he would arrest me. I crept back, ducking out of sight but maintaining a visual of the roof. After forcing EAPPI to leave as well, the captain caught sight of me in the doorway. "You. Come here," he demanded.

"It's okay. I'll leave now," I said, turning to head down the stairs. I wish the threat of arrest could be a nonissue for me. But I want to return to Palestine. If the soldiers arrest me, my likelihood of getting back in the country would drastically decrease. Because of this, they have the trump card. We hold out as long as possible, but when the soldiers move forward to take us, we must leave. Our Palestinian partners counsel us that getting arrested does nothing to help their situation. Nevertheless, I do not like being handcuffed, physically or metaphorically.

The soldiers and police made the settlers leave. Only a matter of time, however, until they return. While still mindful of all the Palestinians who cannot escape occupation, I cannot help but experience relief when I think about leaving CPT Friday. These two months have been exhausting. I am ready to move on—for now.

19

The Next Stage

Thursday, March 1, 2012—Hebron, Occupied Palestine

MARCH IS HERE, WHICH means my time with CPT has come to an end. Tomorrow I leave Hebron and head for Jerusalem where I will meet up with my parents. My mom has come to attend a peace conference in Bethlehem with me during the next week, and my dad comes, as he does each March, bringing six medical school students and residents to do rotations in hospitals throughout the West Bank. During the next month, I will accompany his team to other Palestinian cities suffering under occupation.

I wanted to use this update to reflect over my time with CPT, but I have no idea where to begin. As one friend observed, I may not realize all the lessons learned during this time for weeks, months, or even years to come. For now, I think I will let this experience sit. I want it to simmer relatively undisturbed for a while. This next month should be slower and less overwhelming than the last two. During this time, I hope to quietly meditate on the significance of these last two months. When I return home in early April, I will try to look back over my time here in Palestine and write a comprehensive reflection—if possible.[1]

I end these two months in Hebron exhausted and overwhelmed by what I have seen and experienced. I hate to leave the friends I have made here, but I am grateful for the chance to spend a week with my parents and

---

1. This reflection appears in this book as the epilogue.

a month with my dad and his group. I have eagerly anticipated this transition and am relieved to have the opportunity to move on from Hebron. I leave Hebron grateful for the time spent here, changed by the experience in ways I do not yet fully understand, and excited for this next stage of the journey.

20

The Conference, Hebron, and Israel's "Security Fence"

Monday, March 12, 2012—Jerusalem

I FINISHED WITH CPT over a week ago now. Overcoming the obstacle of heavy snowfall, I reunited joyously with my parents last Friday. The relief I felt to see their faces here was immense, as if a load fell off my shoulders. A sense of refreshment at returning to Jerusalem with my family replaced the suffocation I often experienced during my two months in Hebron.

During this past week, we toured Jerusalem with Dad's medical group, floated in the Dead Sea, climbed Masada, visited Jericho, attended a peace conference in Bethlehem, and walked around Hebron. On Wednesday, Mom and I met Dad's group at the Princess Alia government hospital in Hebron, and I guided them through the Old City, showing them the CPT flat and introducing them to many of the areas and people I wrote about in my previous letters. To be able to show my parents where I have been and to provide them with a glimpse of the thick tension of Hebron life was undeniably the highlight of the week for me. In addition to the warm welcomes and embraces they received from my many friends in the city, they also witnessed the frustrations of arbitrary ID checks, the hassles of checkpoints and bag searches, and the aggression of settlers.

As we stood in the seldom trafficked street that runs by the Qeitun checkpoint, a car full of young settler men drove toward us. Because we did not move out of the way with enough haste, they stopped the car, rolled down the windows, and began shouting at us, eyes wide with anger. The car crawled forward as the young men continued hurling curses our way. Frustrated, I motioned for them to move on, saying the first phrase that came to mind, "*Yalla, yalla.* Hurry and go." This was a terrible decision on my part. Far from being de-escalating, this fanned the flame of their indignation for two reasons. First, it was a dismissal. Second, it was a dismissal in Arabic. The moment I spoke those words, their car jerked to a halt and reversed. I turned to the group and instructed them to calmly but quickly start backing away. Thankfully, the young men did not exit the car. Once they finished shouting their profanities and intimidations, they sped away.

We left Hebron crammed in a taxi van, nine people on seats meant for seven. Once outside the city, we sped toward Route 60, one of the major highways running north to south through the West Bank. Before we reached it, though, a neon baton up ahead waved back and forth, motioning for us to stop. Our Palestinian driver pulled the van to the side of the road, and two Israeli soldiers approached. They asked our driver a few questions and then instructed him to turn off the car and remove the key from the ignition. The soldiers told all of us to exit the vehicle so they could search it for weapons. After we all piled out into the crisp cold air, we waited while the Israeli *Defense* Force soldiers conducted their *security* search, outside a *Palestinian* city, in the *middle* of the West Bank. When the search was complete, I asked one of the soldiers, "Everything OK with the car?"

"Yes, everything's fine," he replied matter-of-factly.

"Do you often find problems when you search cars?" I inquired, my face surely red from frustration.

"Sometimes we find knives," he nodded. I found it fascinating that Palestinian civilians carrying knives in their cars or even on their persons pose such a threat to Israeli national security that random checkpoints in the middle of the West Bank are considered necessary. I wondered how many settlers drive through the West Bank with far more than knives in their cars, given that Israel permits them to carry high-powered weapons at any time. A few days before I left CPT, I saw a settler family walking by the Gutnick Center, a father and mother enjoying the pleasant sunshine, pushing their baby in a stroller. From the father's shoulders hung an M-16.

Meanwhile, soldiers search the bags of young Palestinian children and pull over Palestinian cars along West Bank roads looking for knives.

Mom and I spent most of the week at the "Christ at the Checkpoint" peace conference in Bethlehem.[1] Each day, we took taxis from the home of our dear friends, Abu and Um Shadi,[2] to the Intercontinental Hotel where we listened to lectures on peacemaking and reconciliation, paths to justice and equality through nonviolence, and theologies of the land to combat the dangers of Christian Zionism. We heard from such folks as Shane Claiborne, Ron Sider, Tony Campolo, Gary Burge, and Stephen Sizer, as well as numerous Palestinian activists and theologians like Munther Isaac, Salim Munayer, Jonathan Kuttab, and Alex and Sami Awad. Each encouraged us to take the words and example of Jesus seriously and not seek a zero-sum resolution to the conflict. I was challenged and encouraged to hear from Palestinian Christians who wrestle daily with Jesus's teachings to love our enemies and not to resist the evil-doer with violence. If those who suffer these injustices every day can work hard to look without hate at their oppressors, if they can seek creative alternatives to the downward spiral of violence, if they can practice forgiveness rather than revenge, then *surely* I can do the same.

The conference appropriately took place in the shadow of the Separation Wall (what Israel and Western media often call the "security fence"). This large, concrete Wall slashes into Bethlehem and much of the West Bank, dividing it from Israel, separating Palestinians from their own farm land, and severely restricting the mobility of West Bank residents. Israel claims to have designed and built the Wall to act as security barrier, with the intention of drastically decreasing the rate of suicide bombing by Palestinian extremists within Israel's borders. While a surface glance at statistics of suicide attacks might seem to confirm Israel's declared motive, closer analysis (or a visit to the West Bank or Gaza) shows that ulterior motives must be at work here.

Israel began building the barrier (that is, the Wall and an electrified, razor wire fence) in 2002 along the border of the Green Line, the only internationally recognized border between Israel and the West Bank. But the construction of the barrier quickly detoured from its originally stated

1. For more on this biannual conference, see its website: www.christatthecheckpoint. com

2. This means, essentially, "parents of Shadi." In Arab cultures, the terms *Abu* and *Um* often precede the name of their eldest son. The designation is used affectionately by family and friends, though it in no way officially replaces the parents' given names.

course, making significant darts *into* Palestinian land. B'Tselem, an Israeli human rights organization, estimates that upon the barrier's completion, nearly 10 percent of the West Bank, including 60 settlements, will fall on the Israeli side of the 1967 borders.[3] The barrier as it stands now does not follow any clearly defined internationally or nationally recognized border, with 85 percent of the barrier running *into* the West Bank, away from the Green Line.[4] When the barrier is completed, it will surround tens of thousands of Palestinians on three sides and many on all four sides, totally enclosed inside their own land.[5]

The barrier separates many Palestinians from their land, a devastating situation since land cultivation is one of the primary means for Palestinians to provide for their families. B'Tselem documents that, in total, including East Jerusalem, the Wall directly and physically affects the lives of nearly half a million Palestinians.[6] The current and projected route of the Wall and razor wire fence is telling, as its length is *more than twice* that of the only recognized border. To illustrate, if I wanted to build a fence between my land and my neighbor's so as to keep their dog from attacking my small children or tearing up my lawn, I could build that fence on the boundary line between our two properties. But if that fence deviated into *their* yard, encircling my neighbor's brand new motorcycle, beautiful flower bed, productive vegetable garden, and clear blue swimming pool, one might question whether I am trying to keep the dog out, or whether I am using that claim as a method for taking the motorcycle, flower bed, garden, and swimming pool. I believe this is the logic of the barrier.[7]

No matter how many times I come, no matter how long I stay, and no matter how much I read, write, and speak about the occupation when I am home, I am still shaken by the reality of the Wall. Each time I visit, I have moments where some all-too-familiar aspect of the occupation re-astounds

3. B'Tselem, "Separation Barrier," paragraph 11, lines 3–6.

4. Ibid., paragraph 4, lines 1–2.

5. For a revealing visual of the barrier, see "Restricting Space in the oPt: Area C Map," created by the UN OCHA oPt (www.ochaopt.org). Follow the black line to see the barrier's current and projected path.

6. B'Tselem, "Separation Barrier: Statistics," Table 4.

7. This metaphor is a variation of one used in the excellent documentary *With God on Our Side*. The correlations to the Israeli-Palestinian conflict are not exact, as I certainly mean to make no comparison whatsoever between Palestinians and dogs. I have heard many Israeli settlers make such a comparison, however, as they shout denigrating phrases like, "Each Arab dog shall have his day!"

me, as if I am seeing it again for the first time. Sometimes it's the check-points. Other times the settlements. But *every* time I look up at the ugly concrete barrier towering over all who pass by, I am sickened. To hear the stories of families divided by this Wall, to see the forlorn faces of those who can no longer care for their land because the Wall separates them from it, and to know that U.S. tax dollars have funded its construction leaves me weakened and angry. In Bethlehem, amongst the prophetic, creative artwork decorating the Wall's façade, one can see the words "Made in the USA" boldly stamped every few meters.

We leave now for Qalqiliya, a city surrounded on three sides by Israel's "security fence."

21

Qalqiliya

Friday, March 16, 2012—Nazareth, Israel

AS WE SAT DOWN to dinner upon our arrival to the UNRWA hospital, one of the doctors greeted us, "Welcome to Qalqiliya, the world's largest jail." As we would learn during our three days in this city of fifty thousand Palestinians, seeing Qalqiliya as a "jail" does not require a wild imagination. Israel's "security fence" surrounds it on three sides, with the only opening being a narrow stretch along the main road entering the city. On Thursday, we hired a private van to tour the city, stopping several times to see the Wall, the electric fence, and the checkpoint into Israel, all the while hearing the tragic stories of the Palestinian reality. As Allyson (one of the medical students) vented after only our third stop, her voice heavy, "This is just depressing."

During the Wall's construction around the west side of Qalqiliya between 2002 and 2003, Israel placed the city under curfew and closure. Residents could only leave their houses during certain hours of the day, and only received permission to travel outside Qalqiliya for grocery shopping every eight to ten days. Our local guide, a lifetime resident of Qalqiliya, told us there was a shortage of everything during this time. Israel allowed little into the city and even less out. Once the Wall blocked off Qalqiliya to the west and the electric and razor wire fence hedged it on the north and south, Israel controlled all access in and out of the city. The eastern road could be closed at any time Israel chose, effectively incarcerating the residents in the open air prison of their own city.

Like grasping fingers, Israeli settlements run alongside the northern and southern hills of Qalqiliya, grabbing more land for Israel. The "security barrier" cuts into Palestinian land around Qalqiliya, complicating mobility and usurping real estate as it winds around the settlements, pulling them back into Israel *de facto*. This system of barriers separates Palestinian farmers from their land. The farmers must obtain special permission from Israel, which is often denied, to go work their own soil. They can only get to their farm land through one gate, which opens briefly three times per day. If a farmer misses one of these short openings, he is out of luck. Our guide said many farmers have had to camp on their land because they did not reach the gate in time to return home. Under Israeli law, Israel can confiscate all land that has gone unused for five years. Thus, separating families from their land and denying them access tends to serve well the interests of Israeli expansion.

As our guide pointed out, one of Qalqiliya's major attractions for Israel is its placement, sitting atop one of the major water sources in the region. Once it gained control of the area, Israel began building deep wells around the city, causing the water supply beneath Qalqiliya to drain into the Israeli wells. Israel then uses that water for itself and its settlements throughout the West Bank. In the hills nearby, Bedouin villages sit beside Israeli settlements. The Bedouin often do not have enough water to grow the food they need to eat; the settlements have swimming pools and green lawns.

Water is one of the major issues in the Israeli-Palestinian conflict. Regarding "peace" negotiations, there are five "Final Status" issues that must be resolved: the status of Jerusalem, the right of return of Palestinian refugees, borders, settlements, and water. As detailed in an international legal study funded and coordinated by the government of South Africa in May 2009 (in which the South African government concluded that Israel was practicing both "colonialism and apartheid" against the Palestinians), Israel diverts all of Palestinian Jordan River water and nearly 90 percent of Palestinian ground water to the State of Israel and the settlements.[1] The rest of the ground water is distributed back to the 2.5 million Palestinians living in the West Bank, who—while receiving only around 10 to 60 liters of water per day, much less than the 100 liter *minimum* set by the World Health

1. Francis M. ReMillard summarizes this 300-page study in his pamphlet *Is Israel an Apartheid State?*

Organization—often must pay "four to twenty times more for water than Jewish settlers . . . [who] enjoy 274 to 450 liters of water per day." Israel disables Palestinian access to water by destroying wells, cisterns, pumps, and irrigation systems. Since the occupation began in 1967, Israel has not granted permission for one single Palestinian well to be drilled over the Western Aquifer (where Qalqiliya sits). The use of the Jordan Valley's water resources exclusively for the settlers breaches international law, which limits the occupying state's usage to military needs and prohibits discrimination between residents of the occupied area.[2] B'Tselem estimates that over 10 percent of the West Bank's Palestinian population is not connected to a running water network.[3]

Standing at the checkpoint, I felt as if I was back visiting Nashville's maximum security prison, with tall electric fences, concrete walls, rolls of razor wire, sniper towers, and metal gates. Each morning, nearly four thousand Palestinians (mostly men) line up at 3 a.m. in order to cross over into Israel for work at 6, some to regular jobs, and some unsure if they will find employment. The lines often crawl, as soldiers do not always seem to be concerned with the Palestinians' schedules. Sometimes the soldiers shirk their duties, choosing instead to relax while the Palestinians wait. I personally have walked through these humiliating checkpoints and witnessed soldiers texting, playing games on their phones, reading, or even sleeping. I have observed this negligence both while Palestinians have stood waiting in ever expanding lines, and also at times when Palestinians have passed *through* the security checks undeterred, neither situation to be expected at checkpoints said to be crucial to national security.

For the past two years, I have visited with a group of incarcerated men at Riverbend Maximum Security Institution in Nashville. Behind the walls and razor wire fences, we discuss, contemplate, laugh, keep silent, and practice common prayer. Some of these men are older, but some are young, much too young. One of my friends is probably just over thirty years old and staring down a fifty-year sentence for murder. Another faces two life sentences. Some of the most intense feelings of disillusionment and hopelessness I have experienced have come sitting across the table from my brothers in prison, knowing I can walk out of the gates and go home, but they will never leave. If I ask them, though, what it is like to be incarcerated,

2. B'Tselem, "Water crisis: International Law and the Water Crisis in the Occupied Territories."

3. B'Tselem, "The Water Crisis: Statistics," Table 3.

to be forgotten by society, most of my friends, despite the terrible loneliness and acknowledgement of the broken prison system, will respond, "We put ourselves in here. We made terrible decisions, and now we are paying the price for our actions." They accept the consequences of their choices. The only offense of the people of Qalqiliya is that they are Palestinians living over a major water source.

As we left Qalqiliya and the West Bank and returned to Jerusalem, I remembered a poster hanging in the Bethlehem checkpoint. After Palestinians have stood in line for hours in that cage, experienced humiliation and harassment, they must pass a poster at the checkpoint's exit which reads, "Israel—Where It's Vacation All Year Round."

22

The Mount of Beatitudes
and the Nonviolent Teachings of Jesus

Saturday, March 17, 2012—
Mount of Beatitudes, Galilee, Israel

"Blessed are the poor in spirit, for theirs is the kingdom of heaven. Blessed are those who mourn, for they will be comforted. Blessed are the meek for they will inherit the earth. Blessed are those who hunger and thirst for righteousness, for they will be filled. Blessed are the merciful for they will be shown mercy. Blessed are the pure in heart, for they will see God. Blessed are the peacemakers, for they will be called sons of God. Blessed are those who are persecuted because of righteousness, for theirs is the kingdom of heaven. Blessed are you when people insult you, persecute you and falsely say all kinds of evil against you because of me. Rejoice and be glad, for great is your reward in heaven, for in the same way they persecuted the prophets who were before you."—Matt 5:3–12

Jesus spoke these words here, in these Galilean hills. Perhaps even on the very hill where I sit now, overlooking the Sea of Galilee and the hills of Golan.[1] The water is still. The breeze is gentle but steady, rustling the leaves and allowing the birds to hover in place as they fly. Below me lies

---

1. The Sea of Galilee is referred to as *Lake Tiberias* in the map in the back of the book.

Capernaum, the home base for Jesus during his Galilean ministry. Some of the stone ruins date back to the first century, to Jesus's day. Tourists flock from all over the world to walk where Jesus walked. We want to see the stones that Jesus would have seen, that he would have touched, would have walked on. We want to know, without any doubt, that we have stood where Jesus stood. Unfortunately, as my grandfather, Dr. John McRay—a retired biblical archaeologist and New Testament professor—has told me, not many places (if any) exist around here where we can say with absolute certainty Jesus would have stood, and as I sit here in the garden on this hill, looking out at the calm, blue waters of the lake, I suddenly feel that none of it *really* matters. Whether the stones date to Jesus or not seems irrelevant to me at the moment. Stones and landscapes will pass away, falling prey to the inevitability of nature's evolution and humanity's wars of destruction. They will not last forever. But the piercing words of Jesus, spoken here, will always remain. And they are entirely relevant.

As I watch tourists come and go in massive buses, all wearing matching hats or rain jackets, I am struck by the irony of it all. Jesus delivered his "sermon on the mount" to a people living under occupation from a foreign power. His audience *knew* oppression, almost in the intimate, biblical sense of the word. The people on this hillside slept in oppression, dined in oppression, shopped in oppression, raised children in oppression, died in oppression. They knew it personally. Here today, in this same land, another people know oppression. Another people know occupation. Jesus taught nonviolent resistance and reconciliation to the people in these hills, providing them alternatives to victimhood, violent retaliation, and disengagement.

Today, those who claim to follow this native from Nazareth travel here in flocks to see the ancient stones, to ride boats across the Sea of Galilee, to walk the Via Dolorosa. We come to see where Jesus walked, but it seems we often forget what he taught. We see the places but do not hear the words. Jesus's teachings on this mount are just as relevant today as they were when he first uttered them. I sigh deeply when I drive through the land and see numerous buses belonging to large evangelical Christian groups who are major proponents of Christian Zionism, often donating millions of dollars each year to Israeli settlements.[2] These pilgrims and many others come looking for a "spiritual" experience. And this is important to be sure. I, too,

2. For a fantastic exploration of Christian Zionism, see Porter Speakman's film *With God On Our Side*.

have been the tourist. I have seen the sights and walked the walks. But if we divorce the political message of Jesus from our spiritual pilgrimages to the places where he spoke those words, then I daresay our spiritual journeys are meaningless. In fact, our "spirituality" may be the very thing prohibiting our engagement with the world. We let ourselves off the hook believing we are good Christians because we are "spiritual." We made the pilgrimage to the Holy Land; we say the right prayers; we read the Bible; we have the emotional experiences. But all the while, the battle outside rages. The poor and the "other" are still marginalized and oppressed. Our "spirituality" does nothing for them. I am reminded of a well-known poem usually attributed to an anonymous author, playing off a passage in Matthew 25, which reads:

> I was hungry, and you formed a humanities group to discuss my
> hunger.
> I was imprisoned, and you crept off quietly to your chapel and
> prayed for my release.
> I was naked, and in your mind you debated the morality of my
> appearance.
> I was sick, and you knelt and thanked God for your health.
> I was homeless, and you preached to me the spiritual shelter of
> the love of God.
> I was lonely, and you left me alone to pray for me.
> You seem so holy, so close to God,
> But I am still very hungry—and lonely—and cold.

We have a responsibility to our neighbor. In the parable of the Good Samaritan (Luke 10:30–37), Jesus turns all our notions of neighbor upside down. In the documentary *With God On Our Side*, theologian Stephen Sizer explains that Jesus places the principle conundrum right at the beginning of the story. He tells the expert in the law that the man lying on the road was stripped of his clothes and lying half dead—that is, he is naked and unconscious. Those who pass by, therefore, cannot identify the man's social or ethnic group, not by his dress or his accent. They do not know if he is part of their group or one of the "others." He is just a man, lying on the road, a human being, plain and simple. So this is Jesus's question: "The man on the road is not one of 'yours'; he is not one of 'theirs.' He is a human. Are you going to help him?" Then, to make matters more complicated, Jesus tells the story so that the one person who does the right thing and helps his naked and broken neighbor is the one person the expert in the law would least expect: the "other," the foreigner, the "dirty" Samaritan. This so bothers the expert in the law that he cannot even acknowledge the Samaritan but rather responds to Jesus's question of "Who was the neighbor to the man?" by saying, "The one who had mercy on him." Jesus's words are few: "Go and do likewise." We cannot separate our spirituality from our obligation to our neighbor.

The Mount of Beatitudes is an amazing place to contemplate the Sermon on the Mount. Everything is peaceful and quiet. Actually, as I write that phrase, "peaceful and quiet," I am struck by their frequent companionship. So often, we put those two words together. When all is quiet, there is peace. But I have found that this is not always true, perhaps even rarely so. Insofar as peace entails the absence of the noise of war, then yes, quiet is peace. But nights in Hebron often were still, yet peace remains distant. As I have said before, I think of peace in the biblical term of *shalom*, calling forth images of wholeness and good creation. Nations speak of peace treaties, often referring to agreements that end violence, but whereas the cessation of violence is crucial to the path to peace, ceasefires are not the realization of wholeness, of new creations. Much work must still be done. As of this moment (perhaps I will think otherwise in a few minutes since my thoughts are very much in flux), I am not even sure peace must entail the absence of conflict. Conflict, if handled well, can be beneficial. The difference between conflict within peace as opposed to without is that the conflict can lead to growth and transformation rather than reduction and destruction.

Thus, I consider peacemaking to be a broader pursuit than simply nonviolent direct action. Pursuits that endeavor to heal communities and bring life into dying places are all aspects of peacemaking. I regard my time spent with the Al Basma Center for the Developmentally Disabled in Beit Sahour in 2010 to be just as valid a peacemaking pursuit as my time spent in Hebron with Christian Peacemaker Teams. I am not yet convinced that I have been "called" to any particular avenue of peacemaking, but I am absolutely convicted that as a Christian, I am called to be involved in the hard work of peacemaking and reconciliation, wherever I am and in whatever way I can. I am not yet sure what path I will take, but for now, I am compelled by the issues here in Israel and Palestine, and by the issues in my current city of Nashville, dealing with the injustices of the prison system, reconciliation between victims and offenders and whites and blacks, and the disparity between the housed and the unhoused. Perhaps I will find other paths of peace and justice to pursue, but for now, I am compelled by the whispered promptings of these places.

To return to and expound on an earlier strand of thought, during my time here in Palestine, I have become more and more convicted of the political relevance of Jesus. To clarify, when I say political, I am in no way referring to contemporary partisan systems. I mean no reference to campaigns, or voting, or lobbying. Ethicist and theologian John Howard Yoder spoke of political in a radical way (radical in the sense of returning to the root of the word). The Ancient Greek word *polis* meant *city*, therefore in its classical definition, *political* means "pertaining to the ordering and arrangement of the human community."[3] To say, then, that Jesus is "political" means that Jesus has much to do with the affairs of people, the structure of our lives, the way we spend our time, etc. Too often, we confine Jesus's life and teachings to the "spiritual realm," saying they are "other-worldly." We say that Jesus brought only a "spiritual salvation," and his talk of "the kingdom of heaven" refers to the spiritual kingdom of God. But Jesus said that the kingdom of heaven is at hand, here, among us now. To relegate Jesus's teachings to the category of spiritual ideals or intentions is to allow ourselves a way out, an escape hatch so that we do not have to confront the life-altering implications of passages like the Sermon on the Mount.

As I rest on the rocks in this garden, the Church of the Beatitudes just behind me, three passages jump out to me due to my experiences here the last twelve weeks: Matthew 5:21–25, 38–48, and 7:1–6. Throughout these texts, Jesus teaches practices of reconciliation and nonviolence. "You have heard that it was said . . . but I tell you . . . ." Jesus gets at the heart of the Hebraic law by bringing the law to its fulfillment.

"You have heard that it was said, 'Eye for eye, and tooth for tooth.' But I tell you, do not resist an evil person (with violence). If someone slaps you on the right cheek, turn to him the other cheek also . . . If anyone forces you to go one mile, go with them two miles."[4] (Matt 5:38–39, 41)

Just as the law of "eye for an eye" meant to *restrict* the possibilities of retribution rather than arbitrarily *define* a standard of justice, so too Jesus limits retribution by saying not to resist evil with evil, violence with violence. (Parents often teach their children, "You can't fight fire with fire," but

---

3. Camp, *Who Is My Enemy?*, 29.

4. I add the parenthetical because the Greek word for *resist* there is *antistenai*, which is most often used in reference to the violent interactions of armies in the Greek translations of the Old Testament. The word, then, seems to mean more than simply to "resist" evil. Many scholars, such as the late Walter Wink, feel "do not violently resist an evil person" is the more accurate translation. For more on Wink's explanation, see http://www.cpt.org/files/BN%20-%20Jesus'%20Third%20Way.pdf.

it seems many of us do not really believe this, as we often support the wars of our respective nation-states. Isn't fighting fire with fire—or preventing fire with fire—the basic logic of war?) And in restricting (or actually eliminating) retributive violence, Jesus opens wide the possibilities for creative peacemaking, as demonstrated in the subsequent verses of Matthew 5.

Speaking to a people living under occupation, Jesus addresses their particular situation with ideas for non-passive resistance. In a world where most people are right-handed, for someone to strike you on the right cheek required them to slap it with the back of their hand, an act asserting authority and superiority. You hit your *equal* with your fist, right hand to left cheek. If a slave owner slapped his slave with the back of his hand, the owner was insulting the slave's humanity by demonstrating that the slave was not worthy to be hit as an equal. When Jesus instructs the people to turn the other cheek, he is rejecting the two classic responses: fight and flight. He is telling those gathered, "When someone humiliates you and attacks your humanity, do not fight back, and do not run away. Stand firm. Show him your left cheek and make him hit you as an equal. Refuse to accept the humiliation, but rather turn it back on your oppressor. If you cease to be inferior, he will inevitably cease to be superior." Jesus presents a creative *third* way. The same is true with the "second mile" instruction. Legally, a Roman soldier could force a Hebrew to carry his heavy military pack for one mile, but *only* for one mile. The law forbade soldiers to extract any more than one mile's work from a Hebrew. Here again, in the midst of oppression, when the threat of humiliation and harassment was real every day, Jesus offers a way to assert their humanity—just keep walking. Make the soldier plead with you to have his pack returned. Refuse to be the victim. Who knows? Perhaps during that second mile, that occupier might become a friend.

These teachings are still so relevant here in Palestine. People remain under occupation, daily facing humiliation and harassment. Many of them are seeking third ways of resisting. Practicing "third ways" requires imagination and intentionality. If nonviolence is to be effective, we must plan, prepare, and implement creative options for peaceful resistance. We cannot rely on impromptu action, as we may be prone to react purely upon our emotions. During my time in Hebron, I wanted to see more sessions of creative planning for both Palestinian and international solidarity responses to ID checks at checkpoints, spontaneous searches by soldiers, arrests, and settler violence. Granted, creative planning does not guarantee the success of nonviolence, but I personally would rather approach a situation of violence or harassment with numerous ideas for nonviolent alternatives than be forced to rely on whimsical creativity in those moments of intense frustration, tension, and pain. After all, militaries train soldiers meticulously for combat, carefully working through the best strategies. If we claim to offer a viable alternative to the violence of war, should the discipline and devotion in peacemaking be any less intentional?

Jesus continues with another challenge, this one perhaps more unbelievable than the previous: "You have heard that it was said, 'Love your neighbor and hate your enemy.' But I tell you, love your enemies and pray for those who persecute you . . . " (Matt 5:43–44) I love/hate this teaching. I hate it because loving my enemies and the enemies of my friends seems impossible, and so I do not want feel obligated to continue trying. How can I love those who perpetuate evil? But I have also come to love its wisdom as I grow more convinced each day that sustained nonviolence is impossible without this love of enemies. I recently finished reading Gandhi's writings on nonviolence as selected and edited by the Trappist monk Thomas Merton. Gandhi wrote once that, "Unless you have nothing but brotherliness for those that despitefully use you, your resolution that you would stand by the principle of nonviolence through thick and thin will have no meaning." He goes on to say that nonviolence is "impossible without charity—unless one is *saturated* with charity. It is only he who feels *one* with his opponent that can receive his blows as though they were so many flowers."[5] To expect that we can sustain our commitment to nonviolence while harboring hateful feelings toward our attackers is unrealistic.

Yet, I do not believe that loving our enemies means we must feel pleasantly toward them at all times. I love my family, but I am not always happy with them. I do, however, always desire their good. To love my enemies, then, is to want their good, to not wish harm upon them. Perhaps their good is to be confronted with the truth, and then granted the grace for the space of reconciliation and redemption. If my brother saw me attacking someone, I pray he would not pick up a gun and shoot me in the head. Rather, I hope he would appeal to my conscience, knowing this violent act does not define me and believing I have not passed the "point of no return." I believe Jesus calls us to extend this same grace to our enemies. And this is a grace that necessitates intimacy, for to love someone, you must know them.

5. Merton, ed., *Gandhi On Non-Violence*, 82–83, emphasis mine.

Too often, we toss around such platitudes as, "I don't *hate anybody*. I *love everyone!*" But this is as impossible as it is untrue. We cannot love everyone because we cannot know everyone. We tend to think of love as a general disposition rather than a particular pursuit. As singer/songwriter Andrew Peterson puts it in his song *For the Love of God*, "love is not a feeling in your chest; it is bending down to wash another's feet." My parents taught my siblings and me that love was a decision, a commitment. Love is intentional. Thus, we cannot love our enemies if we do not pursue relationship with them, and if not relationship, then conversation, and if not conversation, at least understanding. True nonviolence and forgiveness require the sharing of our stories. Our stories do not absolve us of responsibility, but rather provide the context and fuel necessary for understanding, which is vital to the pursuit of reconciliation. Refusing to try to understand the perspective of our enemy—of the "other"—is refusing to abide by the teachings of Jesus.

"Do not judge, or you too will be judged. For in the same way you judge others, you will be judged, and with the measure you use, it will be measured to you. Why do you look at the speck of sawdust in your brother's eye and pay no attention to the plank in your own eye? . . . You hypocrite, first take the plank out of your own eye, and then you will see clearly to remove the speck from your brother's eye." (Matt 7:1–3, 5)

Forgiveness requires us to see the evil in ourselves and the good in our enemy, to examine the plank in our eye before going after the speck in our brother's. Granted, our brother's eye may contain much more than a speck, and the plank may even be much bigger than our own, but I find this irrelevant. As Will Campbell has said, "We're all bastards, but God loves us anyway."[6] The point I believe Jesus is making above is the necessity of humility. Benedictine wisdom speaks of the twelve stages of humility. One stage is accepting our own insignificance and imperfections. If we start from the assumption that we are terribly flawed ourselves, that we too are bastards, then perhaps we can hope to extend the extra measure of grace to our enemy that we hope they would extend to us. In many ways, violence is a manifestation of the arrogance of power. To be violent is to wield power over another, and to wield power over another is to assume some form of superiority. Nonviolence should not be arrogant or self-righteous, but must rather be pursued out of a humble awareness of our own blemishes and

6. Campbell, *Writings on Reconciliation and Resistance*, 8.

a belief that there is in fact that of God in the other. True nonviolence is impossible without humility.

Of course, the difficulty with all this is implementation. I know I should love my enemies, but what does that look like, right here on the ground in Palestine, or Nashville, or Belfast, or wherever? I know I need to engage my enemy's story, but how? I do not claim to have answers. I do know, however, that this is the immense importance of community. Based on my limited experience, I believe peacemaking and nonviolence are unsustainable pursuits without an intentional community. Within this community, we have the freedom to be vulnerable about our misgivings of the work of peacemaking, and we have the support system that encourages our persistence. We need an intentional community to hold us accountable to the work to which we commit and to join us in the creative processing that is necessary for the practice of nonviolent peacemaking.

These are my reflections today. Perhaps tomorrow they will be different.

23

They Teach Life

Thursday, March 22, 2012—Nablus, Occupied Palestine

THE NEW STONES OF the house do not quite fit in. They are lighter than the worn stones of most of the surrounding Old City houses. One could easily pass by on the quiet street in front of the house and not give it a second thought, perhaps distracted by laughing children playing soccer on the pavement. But we did not just pass it by. I recognized this place from my only other visit to Nablus in 2007, except then, grass grew next to broken stones where this new home now stood. And suddenly, I remembered the story.

In April 2002, over a year into the Second *Intifada*, Israel invaded Nablus. As our guide reminded me Tuesday, the army attempted to take the Old City but could not drive their tanks and jeeps through its narrow entrances, nor between houses as they are built wall to wall. The IDF resolved this problem with bulldozers and demolition gear. Despite the desperate cries of the home's owner, the military demolished the house with the entire family still inside. Crushed beneath the weight of the debris, nine family members died that day, among them three children, their pregnant mother, and their 85-year-old grandfather. In 2007, the home still lay in rubble. Now, a new dwelling stood in its place.

As I stood staring at the house, imagining the terror of that day in 2002, I heard in the back of my mind the opening words of a traditional Irish tune, "The Frost Is All Over":

> What would you do if the kettle boiled over?
> What would I do? Only fill it again.
> What would you do if the cows ate the clover?
> What would I do? Only set it again.

This is the spirit of the Palestinian people. They are a people of re-creation. Israel's policies of apartheid and occupation have failed in their attempt to drive the people from the land by subjecting them to misery and suffering. You cannot beat a people who refuse to be beaten. You cannot destroy a people who are dedicated to re-creation. We visited the compound of a family of soap-makers who have lived and worked in Nablus since at least 1593. After four attacks from the Israeli military, Naseer has renovated his family home using pieces of demolished houses. Dozens of broken doors lean against the walls of his courtyard, now canvases for colorful paintings. As we gathered in his office, Naseer told us, "We are making life out of what Israel has destroyed."

I see this approach all over Palestine. The people refuse to accept Israel's destruction as final. The harder Israel pushes down, the deeper the Palestinians' feet become rooted in their soil. As my friend Atta said, "Israel knocks us down, and we get up. They knock us down, and we get up. This is our routine." (Atta and his family now live in their third home, the other two demolished by Israel.) Whatever Israel destroys, the Palestinians will restore. When the Golani raided Hebron homes in the middle of the night and destroyed the locks, the Palestinians bought new ones. When a settler destroyed dozens of Muhammad's glass products in his Old City shop, he started over the next day. When the military uproots olive trees, the people plant new saplings. Echoing Martin Luther King, Jr., the Palestinians seem to proclaim to Israel, "We will wear you down by our ability to suffer."

I was asked recently to be on a panel for the documentary *5 Broken Cameras*, which tells, through the personal footage of Emad Burnat, the story of Bil'in's nonviolent resistance to the construction of the Wall and encroachment of settlements on their land. As I previewed the film, my stomach tightened at images of Israeli machinery uprooting cherished Palestinian olive trees to make way for the Wall that now invades the community of Bil'in. But then I saw dozens of men and women marching out to their remaining trees to harvest the olives, armed with ladders and buckets.

Israeli forces stood in the groves protecting the "military zone" they created to safeguard the construction of the Wall. Ignoring all orders to evacuate the area, the Palestinians set to work, filling their buckets with olives from trees planted generations before. Even amidst active destruction, Palestinians cultivate life. In response, the soldiers began beating the people, violently arresting many of them.

Rafeef Ziadah, a passionate Palestinian woman with a unique gift for words, wrote a powerful piece of spoken word poetry in response to a journalist who asked her, as Israeli bombs fell over Gaza, "Don't you think it would all be fine if you just stop teaching your children to hate?" Within the rhythms of her verse, she responded:

> *We* teach life, sir.
> We Palestinians teach *life*, after they have occupied the last sky.
> We teach *life*, sir, after they have built their settlements and apart-
> heid walls . . .
> We teach *life*, sir. We teach *life*, sir.
> We Palestinians wake up every morning to teach the rest of the
> world *life*—sir.[1]

This captures my experience. I see the Palestinians teach life. Yes, exceptions exist, but they are just that: peripheral voices. In the three trips I have made in the last two years, I have met and dined with scores of Palestinians. To date, I have not encountered a single person who called for the destruction of Israel or the death of Jews. They simply want to resist being occupied, yearning to live with freedom and dignity, as do we all. The story I witness here in Palestine is not written with hate. I see Palestinians teaching their children farming, or instructing them in the family trade. I see them teaching their children their Islamic and Christian faiths and the need to rely on God. I see them teaching their children the importance of family and community. I see them teaching their children a respect for elders and tradition. I see them teaching their children to pursue education and create more opportunities than they or their parents before them had. I see them teaching their children *sumoud*, steadfastness, the need to stay rooted in their home, the home of their family for generations past. Indeed, *I* see Palestinians teaching their children life.

---

1. For the video of Ziadah's spoken word piece, see http://www.youtube.com/watch?v=aKucPh9xHtM. Ziadah has the gift of prophetic verse. Watch her videos. Buy her album. Hear her words.

If a Palestinian rewrote the opening lines of that old Irish tune, perhaps it might read like this:

> What will you do if they bulldoze your houses?
> What will we do? Only build them again.
> What will you do if they tear down your trees?
> What will we do? Only plant them again.

24

The Standoff

Saturday, March 24, 2012—Jerusalem

THEIR VOICES GREW LOUDER, neither individual conceding their position. The line gradually lengthened at the Qalandia checkpoint outside the West Bank city of Ramallah, one person after another forced to wait as the verbal confrontation escalated between the young female Israeli soldier and the older Palestinian man. Dad had returned to Qalqiliya for a medical conference, so I was guiding his group back to Jerusalem after our one-night stay in Ramallah. Dragging suitcases and lugging heavy backpacks, we had entered the iron bars of the checkpoint's passageway to find a standoff. The Palestinian man held in his hand authorized written permission for travel, but the Israeli soldier held all the authority. Over the next fifteen minutes, with my camera recording, we watched the incident unfold, grateful that the two shouted in English instead of Hebrew or Arabic.

Their positions were simple: He wanted to visit Jerusalem to pray; she wanted him to return to Ramallah. Despite the Israeli permission paper he waved in front of her, she refused him passage, stating that his permission was "invalid." Back and forth they sparred, he insisting she allow him and his young son to pass, and she insisting they go back. For several minutes, the tensions boiled, like lava ready to explode from a volcano. Then finally, it erupted.

"How can you say I cannot go?" the man exclaimed. "I have a permission!"

"No, you don't!" the soldier shouted back. "You must go back to Ramallah."

The man slapped the permission paper against the window that separated them. "Here is my permission! I have 24 hours."

"No, you must go back!" she ordered again. "These are the rules."

"How are these 'the rules'? I have a permission! You must let me pass! It is Friday and I must go to pray."

"You do not have to pray in Jerusalem!" the young woman snapped back. "You can pray anywhere."

I do not know why her response startled me, as I have come to expect such comments. But to see her prejudice manifested in such disrespect for both her elder and his faith angered me. I very much doubt she would have delivered such a flippant remark to an older Jewish man on his way to pray at the Western Wall. I turned to see the reactions of my fellow travelers. Each face looked stern and tense, heads shaking in disbelief.

Returning my attention to the shouting match, I heard the man declare again, "You cannot send me back. *I have a permission!*"

"I—don't—care!" the soldier nearly screamed, exasperated. "You are not going! Go back to Ramallah!"

Standing firm, the Palestinian man demanded to speak with her superior. To my amazement, she agreed and made the call. Several women in our line migrated to the next security queue, hoping to move along, but that line too stood at a standstill. All eyes stayed fixed on this battle of wills.

After a minute or two, the voice of the young female soldier sounded from inside her monitoring office. "My boss says you have permission, so you can go . . . " I smiled, excited to have witnessed the man's victory. Then I heard the soldier's voice again, " . . . But your son must go back." Apparently, his son, no more than thirteen or fourteen years old, did not have permission to visit Jerusalem. Viewed as a security threat, this young boy accepted 20 shekels from his father (approximately $5) and then passed by me as he walked back through the turnstile toward the exit, head hanging low.

The line began moving again, each person removing all metal and placing bags on the conveyor belt. My turn came, so I squeezed into the turnstile, a backpack on my chest and back, and entered the security area. Placing my bags through the X-Ray machine, I stepped through the metal detector and passed by the window where the confrontation had occurred.

Not only did the soldier on duty (one of five young women sitting in the office) not ask for my passport, she did not even look at my face. We made no eye contact. Just moments after a long, dramatic attempt to deny an older Palestinian man passage despite his permission, I walked through without acknowledgement. I very much wanted to create a scene, loudly insisting that she deny me passage to Jerusalem since I was a foreigner attempting to travel there without written permission. Yet, this protest would only have complicated matters for all present, so I bit my tongue and waited for the others.

Minutes passed with no activity. Allyson had stood directly behind me in line, with Heather, Mike, and Paul trailing her. No one was passing through security. All was still. I moved around and saw that the turnstile was locked with Allyson standing inside. I could hear the giggles of the soldiers in the office as they joked around, playing with each other's hair. All the while, the security area was motionless, and the line grew longer. After ten minutes, the turnstile unlocked and Allyson emerged, her face clinched in frustration. As each member of our group came through, not one had to present their passports. My thoughts jumped to the young boy, finding his way back home alone. I thought of his father, finally permitted to pass after much harassment, despite having written permission from Israel to travel in his own homeland.

And they tell me these checkpoints are for security.

25

Moving On

Friday, March 30, 2012—Beit Sahour, Occupied Palestine

This is it. My time in Palestine is over. After three months in this land, I am leaving. Tomorrow, Dad and I head to the Allenby Bridge to cross into Jordan. Given the nature of my time here, we decided to exit via the bridge rather than Ben-Gurion airport, hoping that security will be less tight since we are not boarding an airplane. Still, I feel anxious. Aside from the risks of humiliating strip searches and lengthy questioning, I risk the possibility of being blacklisted, banned from entering Israel for five to ten years. Some in CPT have suffered this fate. One full-timer legally changed his name so he could reenter. *Inshallah* (God willing), Dad and I can exit without the Border Police knowing of my work in Hebron. If all goes well, we will be in Amman tomorrow evening, and then on to Beirut Sunday morning. There, too, we may have issues, since Lebanon does not allow visitors to enter if they have been in Israel. Once again, we must use clever maneuvering. This weekend could either be fresh and exciting or totally disastrous.

Leaving Palestine this time is different. For the first time in my last three trips, I do not know when I will return. Even if I am not blacklisted, I am unsure when I can come back, as I head to graduate school in Northern Ireland this fall, and my schedule is unpredictable after that. When I said goodbye to our dear friend Mahmoud in the Old City of Jerusalem this morning, I wondered how many years would pass before I sipped tea with him in his antiquities shop again. As I sit here in "paradise"—the apt description our close friends Abu and Um Shadi give to their beautiful home in Beit Sahour—I am reminded of how much I love this place, and how I hate to bid my friends farewell. But it is time to leave. I am ready to be home.

26

The Exit and the Protest

Saturday, March 31, 2012—Amman, Jordan

I HAD MUCH ANXIETY and pessimism about crossing the Allenby Bridge into Jordan, but I did not anticipate what actually happened. Bidding Abu and Um Shadi farewell, Dad and I left Beit Sahour at 7 a.m. and traveled east by service taxi toward Jericho and the bridge. Entering the Israeli security area, we stood in line behind several Arab men and women, all holding Jordanian passports. An Israeli agent walked up and motioned to a few of us foreigners in the back, "You tourists, come." She then led us to the front of the line, bypassing the citizens of the country into which we were entering. When we realized this, Dad and I stopped, motioning to the Jordanians to continue. The man beside us smiled in appreciation and then shook his head in frustration with the agent: "She cannot make like this." Finally, our turn came. The moment of truth.

Dad and I walked up together, hoping our combination would seem less threatening. Dad handed his passport to the agent, who commented on the greatness of Dad's name (David). He inquired about the frequent stamps to Israel in the passport, whereupon Dad explained he was a physician who visited colleagues at Ben-Gurion University in Be'er Sheva and Hadassah Hospital in Jerusalem. A big smile appeared on the agent's face, and he nodded with enthusiasm. Taking my passport, he asked, "You with him?" I confirmed and then waited as he performed the dreaded scan. In

Hebron, soldiers and police photographed me and recorded my passport information on more than one occasion. I feared they had created a file that would flag me at security. The agent looked at the computer screen for a few moments—and then stamped my passport and handed it back to me. That was it. We were through. Dad and I walked away in disbelief. The agent did not ask me one question about why I had been in the country for the last three months. The difference between bridge and airport security is tremendous, evident in that one of our medical group members, who went home early via Ben-Gurion airport after only three weeks in the West Bank, received both strip and thorough bag searches. I, however, spent three months in the West Bank and did not receive one question upon exit. A new wave of energy filled me as we left the terminal and boarded the bus for Amman.

Now, as I sit in our hotel room in downtown Amman, hoping for a restful night's sleep before heading to the airport tomorrow morning to fly to Beirut, I cannot help but notice the unfortunate but fitting end of my final full day in Palestine on Friday. In 1976, Israeli forces killed six Palestinians at a protest against continued Israeli land expropriation. Each year since, Palestinians from the West Bank, Gaza, and bordering countries march toward the Israeli border to commemorate what is known as Land Day. At the invitation of political leader and physician Dr. Mustafa Barghouti, Dad and I decided to go to Qalandia checkpoint in Ramallah Friday, he to work in the field hospital and I to document and, perhaps, participate in the protest. We accomplished only documentation.

We left Jerusalem for Qalandia, passing dozens of armed and armored soldiers and horseback-riding police outside the gates of the Old City. The protest organizers called the event the "Global March to Jerusalem." Given the numbers of Israeli forces personnel and the fact that the West Bank was put under closure the day before the protest, Israel clearly expected trouble. Arriving at Qalandia, we navigated a sea of press, all wearing flak jackets, helmets, and gas masks, a foreboding sign of things to come. Before the soldiers gathered on the main street where the protest was to occur, numerous *shebaab* stood beneath the watch tower of the Wall, hurling stones and glass bottles at the soldiers behind the windows. Protected by bullet-proof glass, metal grates, and concrete walls, the soldiers in the tower faced no threat from the young men's volleys. Yet, as I watched the glass bottles shatter against the formidable tower and saw press dodge ricocheting rocks, I cringed, anticipating that this protest would turn sour quickly. And so it did.

As soldiers moved forward from the checkpoint entrance to the main street, the *shebaab* sprinted for cover, ducking behind a dilapidated building farther down the road. An armored jeep drove up and blasted forth what I have heard called "the Screamer," a pulsing high-pitched noise that pounds the ears and can create severe headaches and disorientation. Over the next twenty minutes, the two groups entered into the usual routine: *Shebaab*, dressed in street clothes and *keffiyehs*, hurled bottles and stones from slingshots and fists; the soldiers, wearing flak jackets, helmets, and shields, retaliated with gunfire, limiting themselves to sound bombs for now, which they shot from their rifles directly at the young men. The explosion of each sound bomb was accompanied quickly by the wailing of an ambulance siren, rushing forward to pluck the injured Palestinian from the fray. Dad waited near the field hospital down the street, next to the beginning point for the official Land Day march; I stood near the soldiers and the tower, filming and photographing yet another lopsided battle.

The march to the checkpoint began an hour after our arrival, starting from the entrance to the Qalandia refugee camp about 250 yards from where the soldiers had positioned themselves. I saw them turn the corner up the road, waving red and orange flags, representing the Popular Front for the Liberation of Palestine and the Palestinian National Initiative, respectively. The *shebaab* continued hurling stones, but the soldiers waited, watching the oncoming mass. Then the march halted. For several minutes, the protesters did not move forward.

But there was this woman.

She emerged from the gathering, dressed in blue jeans and a brown sweater, a red *keffiyeh* wrapped around her face. In her hand, she waved the Palestinian flag, its black, white, green, and red colors flapping in the breeze. She marched forward alone, passing the *shebaab* as she closed the distance between herself and the military line. I walked parallel to her on the opposite side of the street, mesmerized and filming. Behind her, the *shebaab* continued launching stones over her head; in front of her, armed soldiers, a military jeep, and police tank formed an impervious barrier. Leaving the restrictions of my viewfinder, I looked up from the camera to watch her as she reached the soldiers. Without any hesitation, the woman marched up to the prodigious police tank, stuck the Palestinian flag into the metal grate on the front, then turned and walked away. I yelled out in excited support for this act of resistance.

Within seconds, the jeep rolled after her. From its upper canon, it sprayed the horrid Skunk water over her head toward the mass of people beyond. Turning toward the jeep, the woman began to walk backwards, staring into the eyes of the armored beast that crept after her. Then the lower cannon opened, and the jeep spit forth a powerful stream of Skunk water that smacked the Palestinian woman square in the chest. But she did not flinch. She did not run. Holding her pace, she continued walking backwards, facing the jeep as it soaked her head to toe in the revolting chemical liquid. I was awestruck as I witnessed her resistance. Finally, a man ran forward and grabbed the woman, ferrying her off to safety as the cannons rotated right to left, soaking everything within their reach. The breeze carried mist from the Skunk spray onto me, and even that light drizzle reeks enough that I have had to bury everything I wore that day deep in my hiking backpack, sealed inside two plastic bags. That woman will not be able to get rid of the smell for days, but neither can Israel get rid of such courage and *sumoud* as she demonstrated.

The march began moving forward again after the long break in their steps, but the soldiers would have none of it. As if someone flipped a switch, the soldiers sprang from their motionless stance by the tower and charged down the street, launching tear gas canisters into the crowds. Just as quickly, they returned to the tower having successfully disrupted the protest procession. In less than thirty seconds, the now-invisible gas had drifted back down the street in my direction, striking me in the face unexpectedly. Stuffing my *keffiyeh* in front of my face, I took cover in a side alley, hacking repeatedly as my throat and eyes burned. A Palestinian snatched an onion from a garden and handed it to me to breathe through. Soon after, Dad called.

"Where are you?" he asked, voice tense. After I explained my location, he told me to retreat. "It's out of control! The Palestinians are fighting *each other*. They're attacking Dr. Mustafa!" Saying goodbye to some Hebron friends with whom I had just reunited, I hustled up the street toward Dad, weaving through the throngs of angry protesters. Once together, we flagged down a taxi and drove back to Jerusalem.

I learned from Dad that the initial halt of the march, before the Skunk water or the tear gas, was the result of internal Palestinian factions. A news report stated that Dr. Mustafa's group, the Palestinian National Initiative, charged ahead of the rest of the protesters, ignoring the already established plans for a united march.[1] Thus the chaos. Back at the Old City, we heard reports and saw photographs of police at the Jerusalem protest outside the Damascus Gate charging on horseback into the demonstrating crowds as protesters fell beneath the galloping hooves and police on foot beat the people with batons and fists. This reality of overwhelming force from Israel and inner turmoil among Palestinians left me depleted and distraught as we rode the bus from Jerusalem to Beit Sahour for the night. I have felt this way consistently during my three months in the West Bank. I suppose it only makes sense that my last day should have transpired as it did.

Though I am not an expert regarding nonviolent movements, I cannot help but feel that the Palestinian nonviolent movement has much work to be done, in significant part because one encounters great difficultly trying to create a *united* nonviolent social movement in a *disunited* West Bank (not even to mention Gaza), a result primarily of the separation barrier, checkpoints, settlements, and settler-only roads. That being said, I understand—as well as an outsider can—the Palestinian frustration. I have witnessed and, in a very small way, experienced the occupation almost daily for these last three months. Even with the many privileges that accompany the small USA passport book in my pocket, I still dealt with the defeat of arbitrary restrictions on my movement and activities in Hebron. However, as my Palestinian friends often remind me, "You have more rights in our country than we do." I do not know how I would maintain my composure if I lived here as one of the oppressed people. Without creative outlets for this anger, internal conflicts seem inevitable. Unfortunately, these play into Israel's hands because they reinforce the justification of Zionism in the West.

But this is unfair, hypocritical, and perhaps even racist. The United States, while immensely supporting Israel's military, condemns Palestinian violent resistance (or any Arab violent resistance for that matter) to occupation or oppression, imploring the Arab people to pursue nonviolent means.[2] All the while, the U.S. glorifies its own history of revolution, celebrating July 4th with parties and fireworks, a day commemorating freedom achieved after years of bloody, unconventional revolt. Until the United States can look back critically on its own violent history (as well as

1. For the news report, see: http://mondoweiss.net/2012/03/mustafa-barghouti-stable-after-being-struck-in-head-by-teargas-canister-at-qalandiya-israelis-claim-palestinians-attacked-him.html.

2. Part of the problem is that, to my knowledge, the United States has yet to acknowledge the *existence* of the occupation.

its *current* engagements) and imagine alternatives of creative nonviolence, I doubt it has much to say to the Palestinians or any of the Arab countries regarding their forms of resistance.

The West, particularly many Christians in the United States, have bought into the mentality of the necessity of the "perfect victim"—that is, "the other" must be without flaws or vices if we are to promote a cause, support an oppressed people, or reverse a prejudice. Perfect victims are necessary for solidarity, it seems. I have found, for example, that if I try to provide another perspective of Muslims to a person who condemns Islam, I must essentially ignore every problem within Islamic society, because the moment I acknowledge a fault, the conversation ends. The same is true with Palestinians. We Westerns justify our Islamophobia because we have read in the news that stoning still occurs in some Islamic countries, men beat their wives and force them to cover almost every inch of their bodies, and many suicide bombers claim to be devout Muslims. We justify our support of Israel because Palestinians violently attack Israelis (even though the United States most certainly would declare war on Canada or Mexico if either attempted a military occupation). And now look, we might say, the Palestinians are even fighting each other!

But again, this is unfair. Individuals who verbally attack Palestinians, Arabs, Muslims, or those societies seem to forget the profound imperfections in their own countries. Those of us in the United States must exercise great caution before condemning the domestic problems of other nations and societies. Given that the United States has the highest incarceration rate in the world, internal Palestinian disputes should in no way hinder us from advocating for their liberation and the end of the occupation. Those of us claiming Christianity should remember that Jesus said we should first deal with our own faults before we worry about our neighbor's shortcomings. I am not suggesting that the U.S. (or any country in the world) should be flawless in order to offer a voice into the conversation, but rather that the U.S. should not condemn the Palestinians for *their* imperfections. They should not expect flawlessness from the Palestinians or anyone else in order to stand in solidarity with their suffering. In other words, perfection should not be a prerequisite for freedom.

Another aspect of the protests, both in Qalandia and Jerusalem, that stands out is the use of disproportionate and overwhelming force. Soldiers answered rock throwing and chanting with stun grenades, tear gas, rubber bullets, screamers, Skunk water, batons, stampeding horses, and arrests.

The retaliation is so lopsided I do not know whether to laugh or cry. On the taxi ride back to Jerusalem from Ramallah, Dad and I vented to each other about the imbalance of power in the conflict as manifested at the protest we witnessed. Such disproportionate violence is so unnecessary, we thought. As I reflected later, though, I realized that overwhelming power is actually entirely necessary. For Israel to maintain its occupation, it must squash any hint of resistance movements, whether violent or nonviolent. This is why, in 2010, Israel declared all nonviolent protests in the village of Bil'in, a community alive with peaceful resistance against the separation barrier, to be illegal. Israel has created a violent system (as all occupations are), and violent systems must perpetuate violence or they collapse. They are born through violence, and they survive through violence.

I hope for a large-scale, united, Palestinian nonviolent movement not because, in a parade of arrogance, I expect the Palestinians to do what most nations in the world, including my own country of origin, have not done, but rather that, based on the trends of history, overthrowing violence with violence will not bring about the transformation that is needed in this conflicted land. Violence breeds more violence, in one form or another. I believe it always has, and it always will. We cannot fight fire with fire and expect that the fire will die. The first fire will either be replaced with a different one, or the two fires will burn together, producing even more heat. At some point, the cycles and spirals of violence must stop. Because I have both seen the Palestinians' suffering and because I am not Palestinian, I find it hard to condemn the occasional flare-ups of violent resistance to the takeover of their land and the daily humiliation of the Israeli military occupation (and I suspect anyone who, for instance, supports the Revolutionary War, puts "No Trespassing" signs on their land, resents government mandates on the affairs of the people, and would violently protect his or her family from an attacker would have to say the same). Yet, if based only on my study of history and its patterns, I cannot help but believe that, even if violence *could* shake off the occupation, it would not bring about the peace—that is, the wholeness—that most Palestinians truly desire.

At the end of the day, though, I am just an observer, and these are just my thoughts.

27

Beirut

Tuesday, April 3, 2012—Beirut, Lebanon

IT IS POVERTY LIKE you would not believe—nor would you want to. Our medical rounds this morning could not have been more different from our wanderings through Beirut's touristy downtown yesterday. First, we saw the slum, with restless children playing in the narrow, dirt streets; a rudimentary clinic with an open air waiting room, stone-wall seating, and buzzing flies for company; homes created from tin and sheet metal walls, some from cracked, crisscrossing boards and torn cloth, all with roofs of tarps and advertisement banners held down by worn tires; trash heaps along the streets; clothes tied to rusting iron window bars; dilapidated houses near the point of collapse; the stump of an old man's amputated leg, who I'm told is "lucky" to live with only two others in his small room because that space usually holds seven or more. A Palestinian refugee camp came next, with its square, concrete flats stacked one on top of the other, wall to wall with the next precarious set; trash falling from windows onto tin awnings below; a labyrinth of indistinguishable water and electrical cords weaving in and out of each other, up and down the dusty streets; unemployed men leaning against walls, perhaps staring into faded memories of distant dreams; streets only a few inches wider than my wingspan; a prison of despair, where I am sure dreams die before they are even born.

Back in my hotel, I close my eyes and see these images, snapshots of a world I wish did not exist. But it does, and I left that world and came back to the rocky cliffs of downtown Beirut where I sipped cold fresh-squeezed lemonade and gazed at the deep blue waters of the Mediterranean. This contrast disturbs me, and I do not yet know how to deal with that.

28

Homeward Bound

Wednesday, April 4, 2012—Beirut, Lebanon

THE TIME HAS COME to go home. After fourteen and a half weeks abroad, I confess to great excitement to return to my home soil. While I remain disillusioned with the governments and systems (particularly regarding the U.S.) that claim control over our world, I do love the land of my home country, and I yearn to see the green and brown earth of my native Tennessee. My feet long to remain still for a while, to rest and recuperate from a journey of several thousand miles. I really do love travel, experiencing new places and encountering new stories, but the more I travel (with Lebanon making the twenty-ninth country), the more I am convinced that Dorothy was right: "There's no place like home."

I will not try to say anything profound in this final update abroad, but rather simply express my gratitude to each of you who "traveled with me" during these three months. Thank you for allowing me into your homes these last fourteen weeks and for opening yourselves up to the dangers of hearing the other side, the stories "from below," as Dietrich Bonhoeffer wrote. Such stories are indeed dangerous because they threaten our preconceptions and routines of privilege. The more I make myself vulnerable to these "from below" stories, the more some false part of me dies and some new, truer part springs to life. I thank you for opening yourselves to my encounters and reflections and for giving me the opportunity to use you all

as soundboards for my own wrestling with the complexities of this experience. I am truly grateful.

Epilogue
A Myriad of Musings

"WE HAVE FOR ONCE learnt to see the great events of world history from below, from the perspective of the outcast, the suspects, the maltreated, the powerless, the oppressed, the reviled—in short, from the perspective of those who suffer. The important thing is that . . . we should have come to look with new eyes at matters great and small, sorrow and joy, strength and weakness, that our perception of generosity, humanity, justice and mercy should have become clearer, freer, less corruptible. We have to learn that personal suffering is a more effective key, a more rewarding principle for exploring the world in thought and action than personal good fortune."
—Dietrich Bonhoeffer, Germany, 1942

I have found few quotes more important than this one from Dietrich Bonhoeffer. Striving to see the world "from below," an experience Bonhoeffer describes as having "incomparable value," has emerged as a defining pursuit for me, or so I want to believe.[1] As I let this idea, this approach, settle into my life's creed, taking root in my very being, all else becomes affected by its presence, like a drop of dye in a glass of clear water. It changes everything, where I spend my time, how I travel, shop, read history, pursue relationships, and contemplate the mysteries of God. As I explained in the preface, this observation from Bonhoeffer convicts and compels me, and it stood as one of the driving factors in my return to Israel and Palestine in January 2012. I want to keep hearing the stories "from below." I need to hear them. At times during my three months in Palestine, I felt I heard

---

1. Bonhoeffer, *Letters and Papers from Prison*, 17.

these stories *too* well, inundated by their deep power and alarmed at their disturbing frequency.

Some nights, I actually dreamed of soldiers harassing Palestinians. Some dreams were memories, some were new imaginings. Either way, after only weeks on the ground, the violence of the occupation had penetrated even my subconscious. The occupation had occupied my dreams. For the people living daily within this reality, maintaining sanity and calm is an incredible feat. However, like the reporter in Rafeef Ziadah's poem, we in the West so often shake our heads in disapproval at news of more Palestinian violence, wondering to ourselves, "Why can't they just teach their children not to hate?" Aside from making the ignorant assumption that all Palestinians are in fact teaching hatred, we exude a profound arrogance in believing that *we* would certainly "do" otherwise if living under the same terrible circumstances. In our egotism and stubbornness, we fail to see that in the midst of swelling animosity and fear the Palestinians are actually teaching their children something profound—rootedness.

The Palestinian Belonging to the Land

Witnessing the steadfastness of the Palestinians astounds me. This *sumoud*, evident both in their rootedness to their place and their determination not to be defeated by the Israeli military occupation, shocked me in ways I had not experienced before. Palestinian rootedness, clearly marked by their long history in that particular region, has surely been amplified due to the Israeli occupation, for while the occupation pushes down in order to drive out, it has actually embedded the Palestinians more deeply into their earth. The Palestinian resolve appears unshakable. I am reminded of a peaceful protest a Palestinian family held outside their home in Tel Rumeida after their eighth car was torched by nearby settlers. On the charred remains of the vehicle, they placed a sign that read: "We are here . . . not to upset anyone and not to make anyone happy . . . We are here because *we are here.*" The people of Palestine are committed to their place, and this commitment is the very essence of their struggle. Without this resilience to be rooted in the homeland of their ancestors, there is no conflict. They would leave, and Israel would take permanent control of all the land between the Jordan River and the Mediterranean Sea. But the Palestinians will not leave, and neither will the Israelis, and so the struggle and the occupation persist.

Here in the United States, most of us cannot fully understand this commitment to place. We are a people of opportunity, not rootedness. All the way back to the colonization of the Americas, the search for opportunity has been a normative part of U.S. history, providing impetus for the earliest settlers and Western pioneers to the gold rushers and contemporary citizens. Many have called the United States "the land of opportunity." We tend to reside in a place until a more enticing opportunity arises, and then we pursue it without a backward glance. In my own experience, I have really only encountered echoes of Palestinian rootedness in the small towns of the American South, particularly in the rural Appalachian hills of my childhood home. Many families where I grew up have lived in their particular place for generations, some because of conviction and love of place, others perhaps from a fear of the unknown, and still others from a lack of resources. But I have met folk in those hills who, like so many Palestinians I know, would not leave their homes for a small fortune. Those hills are home, and the thought of leaving is incomprehensible.

Such is the case for the Palestinians. More than once, a Palestinian has said to me, "If we left, where would we go? We have always been here." Their lived and remembered histories, their people's narrative, are anchored in the sand and dirt of that place. To borrow a term from John Paul Lederach's *The Moral Imagination*, Palestine is their "ancestral domain."[2] For generations upon generations, their ancestors have lived and died between the river and the sea. Though they now rest beneath the soil, they are still very much alive in the memories of those living today.

I remember one day in Hebron, I visited the home of my friend Muhammad and was met by a seemingly unending banquet of delicious foods. While we dined, Muhammad translated for me the questions his father continued delivering my way. At one point, Muhammad's father explained, "The problem with the people of the United States is that you do not know your history." Having an undergraduate degree in history myself, I pushed back, naively throwing out a few dates and names to prove a sufficient understanding of U.S. history. "No, you did not understand what I said," Muhammad translated for his father. "You do not know *your* history." Perceiving my puzzled look, he continued. "What's your father's name?" David, I told him. "And his father's name and so on?" I told him my grandfather's name is John, and his father was called "Buck," but beyond that, I could go no further. Muhammad translated as his father raced on, "Three

2. Lederach, *Moral Imagination*, 132.

generations? That's all you know, and you have actually studied history!" Starting with his father, he then named at least ten generations back, often even adding their villages of birth. Muhammad's father explained that most people in the United States cannot empathize with the Palestinian struggle to stay in the land of their ancestors because most people in the United States cannot even *name* their ancestors, much less tell their stories or locate their origins.

This anecdote is paradigmatic of the Palestinian belonging to the land. Their souls dwell in that place, buried in layer upon layer of generational stability. Their pasts reside in Palestine, staying always in the forefront of their vision as they fight to stay true to their stories and thus their place. The question of land is not a legal issue for the Palestinians; it has little to do with rights or titles on paper. Rather, the land is the Palestinians, and the Palestinians are the land. They are inextricably connected, for that land is the place of their ancestral stories. Their gardens and orchards are like family. Previous generations planted the seeds of the olive trees that current generations now tend to so that future generations can benefit from plentiful harvests. Their pasts exist in their present and connect to their future. To remove them from Palestine is to separate them from their past. And if you take away a people's past, then the people cease to be, for our histories define us.

Often, however, in pro-Israel circles, particularly here in the U.S., I hear Palestinians referenced simply as "Arabs," a term that effectively separates a particular people from their particular place. In order to promote the idea of an ethnically exclusive Jewish nation-state in historic Palestine, one must delegitimize the belonging the Palestinian people feel to the land, dissolving their need to be there. By simplifying them to the label of *Arab*, supporters of Israel rob the Palestinians of any ties to historic Palestine. The logic goes that Palestinians can find a home wherever other Arab people reside because they are all the same. But they are not all the same. Palestinians differ from Lebanese, who differ from Syrians, who differ from Iraqis, and so on and so forth. This became strikingly clear to me when my dad and I visited Beirut's Palestinian refugee camps. According to many Lebanese, the situation for the Palestinian refugees is worse in Lebanon than in Palestine. Lebanon does not welcome the refugees, legally denying many the opportunities to work in numerous occupations, confining them to poverty and ghettos. Both the Lebanese and the Palestinians want the refugees to return home. Contrary to wishes of Zionist parties, Palestinians cannot just "go wherever other Arabs reside." They are not all the same. The Palestinians belong to Palestine.[3]

This sense of rootedness is one of the major weapons for the Palestinians. As one doctor stated, "This is how we fight"—through fidelity to their roots. In late March, I visited Taybeh with some of the members of the medical group. Twenty minutes from Ramallah by taxi, Taybeh is the location of the only beer brewery in Palestine. During a tour from the enthusiastic foreign wife of the owner, she told us that her husband stays and brews beer as a form of nonviolent resistance. She explained that in the midst of the chaos and oppression engulfing them, the Palestinians need something "normal," something stable. Her husband sees this as his role. Additionally, according to our tour guide, each year's Taybeh Oktoberfest brings together more Palestinians and Israelis than any other event in the country. Local beer provides the space for interaction, for the exchanging of stories. In Palestine, brewing beer is nonviolent resistance. Revolutionary.

Nonviolence and the Teachings of Gandhi

Learning nonviolent resistance from Palestinians stood as one of the most compelling aspects of my time in the West Bank. I had read much literature regarding nonviolence both in my undergraduate years and in my time since, but I had not yet had the opportunity to put my convictions to the test, at least not in situations of intense conflict or physical violence. Reading through Thomas Merton's edited selections of Gandhi's writings on nonviolence during my three months in Israel and Palestine proved most helpful. Perhaps the concept that most compelled me was Gandhi's belief in the importance of self-purification, or the process of creating the nonviolent self.

In my understanding, Gandhi held that strategic nonviolence alone would ultimately prove meaningless. That is, we should not pursue nonviolence solely as means to an end. For Gandhi, *nonviolence* was the end. He believed nonviolence to be the law governing the universe. Everything else was (and still remains) either a footnote or a distraction. Gandhi believed

3. All terminology has its limits. I use the term *Zionism* somewhat broadly here, and thus want to recognize in this note that there are those who claim Zionism but do not promote the expulsion (or deny the existence) of the Palestinians. I have met both Israeli and non-Israeli Jews who claim Zionism but also advocate for the two-state solution, explaining that, for them, Zionism simply entails supporting the right of Israel to exist in historic Palestine.

that though we live as if the law of violence governs us, this is simply an illusion. To illustrate, in the ancient world, many people believed the earth was flat. They spoke as if it was flat, studied as if it was flat, traveled as if it was flat. But of course, it was not, yet they still orchestrated their lives around the belief that the world had edges off which one could sail.[4] The same is true today regarding nonviolence, or so Gandhi seemed to argue. Ostensibly, power (and often thereupon violence) is the law governing the lives of people. We speak, study, travel, and live as if the pursuit of power is legitimate and meaningful. Yet, the law of nonviolence and God Alone structures our world—we just haven't realized it yet.

Thus, Gandhi says we should practice nonviolence for the sake of nonviolence. The task is first to begin the process of creating the nonviolent self. If we use nonviolence only as a tool, we will discard it the moment we achieve (or fail to achieve) our goals. Instead, by pursuing nonviolence within the self, we will then naturally externalize that nonviolence in our interactions with others. This is terribly important to hear. Before we can hope to practice nonviolence with our enemies—that is, our *other*—we must first practice it with our friends, with our family, with our partners. The task is to cultivate a culture of nonviolence in all our circles of interaction, first the inner, then the outer. If we cannot be peaceable toward those whom we know and love, how can we hope to be peaceable toward those we do not know? CPT has adopted this approach within the structure of its organization. In addition to focusing on externalized nonviolence, CPT strives to undo oppressions within itself—namely the oppressions of racism, sexism, and heterosexism. Those in CPT understand the importance of Gandhi's counsel and seek to transform the violence within themselves before confronting the injustices surrounding them.

Reconciliation, Rehumanization, and the Single Story

During my months in Palestine, some of the hardest work I encountered was shaking off the blinders of the single story. Often, I wanted there to be one. Hating the soldiers (or anyone for that matter) is much easier once we buy into the myth of the single story. If I believe all Israeli soldiers to be cruel and heartless (as many portray themselves), I can angrily dismiss them as irredeemable brutes. I knew before I arrived in Hebron to work with CPT that I wanted to be intentional in allowing soldiers to present

4. I thank Richard Goode for this illustration.

a different story. When the moments presented themselves, I tried to embrace the space for conversation.

Often, though, this was impossible, as soldiers frequently harassed Palestinians. During those times—and when I was not fuming—I would attempt something simple, something I anticipate most of our parents taught us from our childhood: I tried to put myself in their position. Knowing my passionate personality (and the fact that I briefly considered joining the military before college), I have little doubt that had I grown up in the intense political, militaristic climate in which these young men and women came of age in Israel, I too would have accepted an M-16 and West Bank placement when I turned eighteen.[5] Had my culture completely immersed me in the history of Jewish suffering and the founding of the State of Israel from a young age, my narrative of formation would greatly contrast my current one. Only naivety would allow me to assume that my story would have sprouted and grown identically when planted within a different context. But beyond this, I could often see in the young faces of some of the female soldiers in Hebron the face of my own cherished nineteen-year-old sister, Anna. What manner of grace would I extend to her if she wore the IDF uniform?

Witnessing nonsensical, unprovoked harassment day after day, however, stirred feelings in me that I found difficult to transform. Watching an armored soldier aggressively arrest a young child for allegedly throwing a stone, I knew who the "bad guy" was. I felt justified in my anger toward the armed aggressor. And perhaps I was. Anger at injustice is not wrong, but rather *can* be the spark that compels us towards constructive social change. I resonate with this line of a beautiful Franciscan prayer: "Bless us with anger at injustice, oppression, and exploitation of people, so that we may work for justice, freedom and peace." Anger can be transformative, if channeled constructively. However, if we try to make our anger persist, it can also prompt us down the path of destruction, leading us to practices of dehumanization and retribution. This continues to be an essential struggle for me: learning how to channel my anger at injustice so that I pursue journeys towards peacemaking and reconciliation rather than retaliation and deeper division.

5. While Israel requires all male and female citizens, save for a few exceptions, to join the military, a movement is growing of Israelis who refuse to participate in military occupation. They are known as refuseniks. For more, see Carey and Shainin, ed., *The Other Israel.*

If I have come to any firm conclusions during my travels, it is this simple fact: Our world is terribly broken. Earth is full of unfathomable and unjust disparities. Beyond just the lucky (or cruel) accident of birth, humanity is divided through intentional separations, whether based on color, gender, religion, economics, ethnicity, sexual orientation, etc. We live in a world obsessed with the surface. My Western culture is fast-paced, always on the go. We try to cram as much into the limited hours of a day as possible. We have grown accustomed to immediate accessibility, instant results, and ready-made commodities. This is why reconciliation, love of enemies, service to the *other* often feels foreign, or even foolish. Those pursuits take time, requiring intentionality, which is a value our impersonal culture does not seem to hold in high regard. My generation is a technological one, hands always full with our tablets, smart phones, iPods, and laptops. We have become so globally connected, yet simultaneously so locally estranged. We can sit on a park bench video-chatting with someone in Malaysia, all the while avoiding eye contact with the person inches beside us. The long, laborious processes of transformation and reconciliation are tough to preach (and practice) in a world where people do not know how to talk with each other, and who often do not appear willing to take the time to learn.

This is the addictive quality of the single story—it is convenient. Believing in the single story requires no effort; it extracts no energy. We lazily put on lenses that filter our world into "us vs. them," creating a very simple collective identity of the *other*, devoid of all individuality. We minimize their good qualities and exaggerate the bad, while overlooking our own faults and magnifying our strengths. We see "our side" as full of unique individuals, while "their side" is all the same. Is this not the logic of ardent nationalism, especially in times of war? The battle is *always* "us" against "them." The struggle is zero-sum—that is, for "us" to win, "they" must lose. I am reminded of two bumper stickers I saw in northern Ohio. The first read, "Achieving World Peace Through Military Victory," and the second, "Bring the Troops Home After Total Military Victory." Here the logic is stated very succinctly: Peace can exist only after "we" have won, and "they" have lost. Whatever it takes, however *long* it takes, "our" side must emerge totally victorious. We have no desire to know the other side for we assume we already do—they are all the same: evil. Primarily through the profoundly determinative teaching of history, the Powers often spoon-feed us a nationalism that slides down easily, but once it settles inside us, it can metastasize and destroy our decency and human compassion.

A couple of years ago, after making a grocery run at the Green Hills Kroger in Nashville, my college friend Josh Cummings and I were just opening the doors to my car when we heard someone yelling from across the parking lot. After a few seconds, we realized he was yelling at us. I spotted a middle-aged man about thirty yards away, gray hair, goatee, and anger in his eyes. Glaring at me, he shouted, "Free Palestine? Free Palestine, huh?" He was referencing my "Free Palestine" bumper sticker sitting in the bottom-middle of my rear windshield.

"We should go," Josh encouraged as we began to get in the car.

The indignant shopper continued, and I stared at him in disbelief. "You wanna know what we should do to all them Palestinians?" he yelled, and lifting his hand, answered, "We oughta nuke all them bastards!" and he tapped his thumb repetitively against his closed fist as if pushing the nuclear button. I wished him a pleasant day and we drove away, amazed that two words on a car window could evoke such a hate-filled outburst.

This is an example of the disturbingly common single story of Palestinians that I have encountered at home in the U.S. Such hatred grew from the decaying soil of this man's single story that he had seemingly become blind to the consequences of his loathing: that is, due to the intimate geographical proximity between Palestine and Israel (and all the Israeli settlements *inside* Palestine), nuking the Palestinians would undoubtedly take out a prodigious number of Israelis as well, not to mention destroy some of the holiest sites of the world's three largest monotheistic religions, thereupon likely igniting World War III. Such is a result of single stories. For this man, a single story of Palestinians had so poisoned his thinking that no gray existed in his understanding: "all" those Palestinian "bastards" should be obliterated. We must acknowledge, however, that such a monolithic image of Palestinians has been informed largely by media.

Too often, Western media have presented a single story of Palestinians, choosing only a handful of repetitive descriptors, primarily "terrorists." Surrounding images of masked, screaming faces whose hands burn flags and hold Arabic signs (which, of course, we believe could only say "Destroy America" or "Death to Israel"), the articles leave the readers believing that all Palestinians hate the United States and are the sworn enemies of the West and its democracy (as if we assume no justification could possibly exist for a position of retribution against the West's global engagements).

But again, the issue with the single story is not that it is necessarily untrue, but rather that it is incomplete. While some Palestinians *have* engaged in terrorist activities, espoused vendettas toward the United States, and called for the destruction of the State of Israel, I have found these pursuits and perspectives—historically and presently—to be profoundly marginal. Through my numerous trips, I have encountered very different stories of Palestinians, primarily ones of incredible hospitality.

Palestinians are a people for whom welcoming the stranger is a consistent beat in the rhythm of their lives. In my experience, Palestinian hospitality is unprecedented, and that is truly saying something coming from a man born and raised in the American South, where Southern hospitality is legendary. More than once, I have met a Palestinian for the first time, within an hour received an insistent invitation to dine in his or her home, and then emerged from the experience barely able to walk due to the generous table shared out of often meager resources. The prevailing judgment from my homeland tells me these people are terrorists, that they desire both my destruction and that of my culture. But my encounters and my relationships tell a different story.

Relationships change our perceptions. They allow us to get close enough to hear each other's pain and see each other's beauty, in all its many complexities. In my visits to Riverbend Maximum Security Institution in Nashville, I have sat around a table with the same group of men since late 2009. A brief write-up in the newspaper would refer to these men as murderers and rapists, and while that is most certainly an indelible aspect of their story, there is much more. There is more that comes before those events in their stories, and I can personally testify that more comes after. But it is only through *respect* that we can come to know this.

Etymologically, *respect* (from the Latin *spectare*) means "to look again." To respect others and their stories, then, means to take another look, refusing to let preconceived judgments and assumptions paint the final picture of their identity in our minds. Respect allows us the potential to transcend our fear, making it possible to embrace the "mystery of peace," which world-renowned peace practitioner John Paul Lederach says is found precisely "in the nature and quality of relationships developed with those most feared."[6] Respect therefore is choosing to engage once more, to ask yet another question, to believe, even if naively, that there is something else, something deeper, something very human and familiar about the *other* now in our

6. Lederach, *The Moral Imagination*, 63.

midst. Without respect, then rehumanization and reconciliation are only pleasant fictions with no hope of realization.

Cornel West is often attributed with saying, "Justice is what love looks like in public." I, myself, continue to find that if we have engaged the *other's* story, if we have intentionally created or serendipitously discovered relationship, then everything can change. Even the very definition of justice may be altered. Relationship with the *other* does not just rearrange the equation, so to speak; it changes the factors, and thereupon the outcome. Our stories intertwine as we pursue relationship.

Then, upon pursuit of these relationships, we soon come to realize two important truths: First, that, as Lederach notes, "ultimately the quality of our life is dependent on the quality of life of others," including even our enemies.[7] A beautiful Irish saying, when translated into English, puts it this way: "It is in the shelter of each other that the people live." Second, that—though we so often (and somewhat inevitably) assume our own interpretations of both ourselves and the *other* are most accurate, we too have a life in the imagination of the *other*. Just as we script their narrative of identity in our minds, so they create one of us in theirs. And in this process of pre-encounter imagining, we have a proclivity towards attributing to our *other* a story without nuance, dictated solely by the reported horrors or disgraces we so readily accept as truth.

Yet, we do not see ourselves as most appropriately identified by our worst mistakes, so why should we identify others this way? Christian history, for example, is filled with many horrific pages, complete with crusades, inquisitions, torture, cannibalism, holocausts, internal wars, cover-ups, terrorism, sectarianism, and colonization. Yet, those of us within the Christian tradition believe (or at least hope) that Christianity is better than the worst things it has done. The same grace must be extended to Islam, Palestinians, Israelis, the incarcerated, or anyone else. The single story is the bane of reconciliation, and it is the propagation of this single story myth for which we must keep a sharp eye on the horizon. To engage the journey of reconciliation, we must work to shorten the distance between "us" and "them," embodying tokens of resurrection and redemption in the broken spaces of our communities and our world.

After I returned home, my sister gave me the novel *The Hunger Games*, the first book in a trilogy by Suzanne Collins that spread like an epidemic. I started reading the 400-page story and, like most readers, could

7. Ibid., 35.

turning the pages. As I followed the dramatic events unfolding for
y's heroine, Katniss, I realized that books like *The Hunger Games*
e-turners not only because of their suspense, but also because the
reader has become inextricably engulfed in the protagonist's story. We keep
turning the pages because we want to know what happens to Katniss, and
we want to know because we have allowed ourselves to become invested in
her story, and now we care. I wonder what would happen if we learned our
enemy's story—the *other's* story—that way. If indeed the enemy is someone
whose story we do not yet know, what would happen if we learned and
invested so much in their story that we felt compelled to "read on," to keep
turning the pages of their narrative? What if we came to genuinely care?

Granted, what we learn of the *other's* story *may be* disgusting, horrid,
and inexcusable, as some stories are. In fact, the more we come to know a
person through his or her stories, the more we may realize just how much
we genuinely dislike him or her. While certainly containing transformative
potential, storytelling will not always lead to positive relationships between
antagonists, especially in instances of prolonged violent conflict or deep
personal trauma. We must be careful to avoid the naivety of assuming
that engaging each other's stories will formulaically lead to reconciliation.
Storytelling is not the recipe, so to speak, for reconciliation, but rather an
essential ingredient as it allows us to reimagine our constructed narratives of both *self* and *other*. Though reconciliation is not always attainable
by engaging the *other's* story, we certainly cannot reconcile without such
engagement.

Reconciliation—the journey toward (re)establishing trusting relationship with our *other*, learning to "live together well"[8] with them—requires
that we come to empathize with each other, that we try to see the intrica-
cies of the world through the *other's* particular lenses.[9] This does not mean
we will agree with or even accept their perspectives, but such practices

8. Theologian Jon Hatch defined reconciliation as such in a university lecture on
community divisions in Belfast: "Reconciliation is the ongoing process of living together
well after violent conflict and in the reality of sectarianism and social division." Tailoring
his definition to the Northern Irish context, what he captures so well in this succinct
description is the importance of reconciliation moving beyond coexistence and entering
into a new realm in which a relationship of trust has developed that allows for positive
connection to continue, even while remaining in the midst of devastating divisions. See
Hatch, "Separation Barriers and Idolatry."

9. For more on this, see Halpern and Weinstein's very helpful article on the role of
empathy in reconciliation, "Rehumanizing the Other: Empathy and Reconciliation,"
561–83.

rehumanize the *other*, restoring to them all the complexity that our stereo-types and prejudices had previously denied them. If, through the process of telling and hearing one another's stories, we come to see the human side of the *other*, then disagreements and differences can become more manage-able and less polarizing. We may learn to live in the tension of the difficult questions that emerge without retreating into our ghettoized preexistences, where clear boundaries divide "them" and "us." We humans tend not to be static creatures, but rather quite kinetic in our intra- and interpersonal dynamics. Rehumanization allows us to acknowledge this human fluidity. It is, in essence, granting the *other* the freedom to be complex.

In the end, reconciliation, even empathy, is not always possible for those who have suffered tremendous trauma. Each particular situation must be addressed independently. Though considering the offenders' stories may be beyond the scope of the victims' or survivors' abilities, the ultimate hope of storytelling within the context of reconciliation praxis is to lend itself to the possibility for healing and transformation. When we tell stories, we cre-ate the space for conversion and are vulnerable to its power. As my brother Jonathan wrote, "In order to overcome old prejudices we must be converted to a new one: the prejudice of love for the other whose face we are now coming to see, whose name we are now coming to understand, and whose story we are now coming to hear."[10]

In Israel and Palestine, however, there is a major roadblock (quite literally) to learning the other's stories: They are separated. The Powers have instituted division, building physical barriers in and around the West Bank and sealing off Gaza. Israel forbids its citizens from entering the Pal-estinian-controlled areas of the West Bank, and it rarely grants Palestinians permission to enter Israel. My father spoke with an Israeli woman visiting Qalqiliya who confessed that she did not meet a Palestinian from the West Bank or Gaza until she was twenty years old. In the film *Encounter Point*, the audience follows an Israeli settler in his *thirties* who meets a Palestin-ian for the first time, though he had lived his entire life in a West Bank settlement, surrounded by Palestinians. For the most part, both peoples see and hear only a single story of each other. Most Palestinians only know Israelis as soldiers, their encounters limited to Israelis clothed in uniforms and holding guns. Many Israelis, like most U.S. citizens, only know Pales-tinians through the news reports, seeing images of rockets launched out of Hamas-controlled Gaza, or stone-throwing *shebaab* at protests. The people

10. McRay, *You Have Heard It Said*, 82.

have little to no opportunity to participate in interactions that challenge the prevailing stereotypes.

This separation, of course, is the essence of apartheid and a necessity for the survival of occupation. False myths can only prevail if people remain isolated from each other. Hatred needs fear, especially fear of the unknown. If people do not remain separated, then this fear of the unknown suffocates. This is why the "security barrier" and the implementation of apartheid (or separation) are crucial for Israel. If Israel allows the people of the land to interact, then it makes room for the destruction of its myth, and thereupon the unjust system built around and upon that myth. Little is more threatening to systems of discrimination and apartheid than an ongoing process of sharing real human stories. Storytelling has great potential to combat fear, but apartheid eliminates this possibility. Keeping people separated allows the Powers to dictate the images the people receive, controlling the representation of the *other*. In the end, both peoples are enclosed, trapped in the confines of the occupation. As graffiti on the Wall at Qalandia so prophetically observes: "One wall. Two jails."

The Necessity of Justice

For all this talk of reconciliation, one thing cannot be ignored, and that is the necessity of justice. The Hebrew scriptures are showered with calls for justice. The writer of Deuteronomy instructs the people not to "deprive the foreigner or the fatherless of justice" (Deut 24:17). The Psalmist speaks of righteousness and justice as the foundations of God's throne (Ps 89:14). The prophet Isaiah delivers the word of God, telling the people to "learn to do right; seek justice. Defend the oppressed" (Isa 1:17). Micah says that the Lord requires acts of justice and a love of mercy (Mic 6:8), and Amos calls on the people of God to "let justice roll on like a river, and righteousness like a never-failing stream" (Amos 5:24). Nearly every book of the Hebrew scriptures either identifies justice as a primary concern of God or calls on God's people to practice it, *particularly* regarding the marginalized and oppressed.

Far too often regarding the Israeli-Palestinian conflict, we gloss over the (sometimes) nasty issues of such justice in order to pursue the warm niceties of "common ground" discussions and "interfaith dialogue." While these surely must not be disregarded, they run the risk of simply providing a sugarcoating for the bitter, difficult conversations concerning justice.

They can become a diversion, a way to avoid necessary confrontations. But systemic injustice must be confronted, ideally through creative, assertive direct action via nonviolence. To remain neutral, to keep quiet, is to in fact give one's voice and support to the aggressor. When in the midst of rampant injustice, apathetic inaction should never be an option. Aggressors and silent bystanders, whether consciously or unconsciously, work together.

In all our peacemaking pursuits, we must actively seek justice. Since differing conceptions of justice certainly exist, it is terribly important that we clarify the term. I think our conversations on justice frequently veer (or even start) off track. Here in the West, we are born and bred within a retributive context, and thus we tend to conceptualize justice within the contemporary framework of our punitive criminal "justice" system. We assume that justice entails a fitting (or proportional) punishment for a certain crime. Looking through our default retributive lenses, we see what we believe justice *is* without asking the important preliminary question, "Where should justice lead us?" It seems to me that the ultimate hope of justice should be to serve as a stepping stone on the path to healing, whether personally, communally, or societally. Injustice divides people from each other, creating rifts in the fabric of society. If our pursuits of justice continue to expand those divisions, then what positive role is justice serving?

Might the lenses of *restorative* justice provide a more compelling vision for our pursuits? Restorative justice believes that relationships, rather than laws, are the ties that bind society together, and thus it interprets the violation of relationships as the principal damage of crimes committed. Justice then entails addressing the harms done and the needs of all involved, naming the obligations of the offenders, providing a space to include the voices of all who have a stake in the offense (that is, victims/survivors, their communities, *and* the offenders), and putting forth an effort, to whatever extent possible, to make things right. The hope of restorative justice is that it takes into account people's stories. Granted, restorative justice may not be the answer to the overwhelming complexities of justice praxis. We must ask ourselves, however, if the systems we rely on today are actually aiding us on our journey toward communities of healing and reconciliation, or rather primarily succeeding in further alienating societies that are already far too willing to expand the gap between "us" and "them."[11]

11. For a very succinct and helpful outline of restorative justice, see Zehr, *The Little Book of Restorative Justice*.

Whereas proposing a system of restorative justice as it relates to Israel and Palestine would require far more space than I am willing to take in this final essay, at the very least justice in Israel and Palestine must mean two things: First, equal rights and access to resources for Palestinians, both those in the West Bank and Gaza as well as the Palestinian minority inside Israel; and second, it must mean the ability to govern one's own affairs, set free from the noose of strangling external impositions. In short, at a very simple yet simultaneously complex level, justice entails ending the occupation. Such a move is in fact Israel's only true hope for security, as it cannot expect to occupy another nation without retaliation. Israel—and its primary ally the U.S.—cannot be satisfied with ceasefires and temporary lulls in rocket attacks and bombing campaigns without offering any intention to deal with the deeper, systemic injustices of occupation and blockade, as is more specifically the case for Gaza. Israel has the right to security, and it is justified in its concern for such. But those who claim unwarranted aggression from the Palestinians must stop fooling themselves that Palestinians have an innate hatred towards the Jewish people and that military occupation and blockade have nothing to do with Palestinian violence. They are entirely interconnected. Justice cannot be overlooked for the cause of sustainable peace.

Thus, we should not talk about true reconciliation between Israelis and Palestinians without simultaneously demanding an end to the occupation. We should not preach renewed relationships without addressing the stories of inequality, oppression, and pain—on both sides of the Wall. Injustice causes division. How can we hope for wholeness while there is still separation? Too often, it seems we fail to understand that confronting injustice is a necessary step on the journeys of peacemaking and reconciliation. Peace, *shalom*, *salaam*, wholeness *cannot* exist without justice for all within its borders. And this is just as true at home in the United States as it is in Israel and Palestine.[12]

12. Authors Allan Boesak and Curtiss Paul DeYoung discuss this in their recent book *Radical Reconciliation*, where they argue that pursuits of reconciliation often neglect to address the deep roots of injustice, frequently resulting positively for the rich and powerful, while denying justice for the poor and powerless. They call this "political pietism," and in the case of the Christian failure to address it, "Christian quietism." Both are unacceptable.

Bringing It Home

One of my most important realizations during my two months with CPT was coming to understand how much work must be done in my home place. I am beginning to wonder to what extent involving myself in Palestine or Northern Ireland or wherever else indicates that I believe, whether consciously or subconsciously, that the state of crisis or humanitarian urgency in the United States is so innocuous that I must work abroad if I am actually to do any real good. Whereas I was somewhat born into an involvement in Israel and Palestine due to my multigenerational family connection to that land, I do not want to make the mistake of oversimplifying the immediacy of the many dire situations at home in the United States.

Though many of us from the U.S. convincingly fool ourselves otherwise, the United States is one of the most violent nation-states on earth.[13] While militarily engaged numerous places in the world, the U.S. also has incredibly high rates of gun violence and incarceration. Prisons are too full. The homeless, in far too many places, are criminalized. Our hetero-normative culture condemns and bullies homosexuals so unrelentingly that young people commit suicide because death is more enticing than growing up homosexual in the United States. And here in Nashville, in my interactions with black friends, I often must only move past the usual superficial chit-chat to hear stories proving racism is still alive and well. We live in a white-male dominated culture, shaped by an overarching historical narrative of white-male supremacy. Minorities are harassed *here*. People are imprisoned unjustly *here*. Peacemaking in Israel and Palestine is terribly important, but if we are not attending to our own streets, our own prisons, our own history books, our own churches, synagogues, and mosques—that is, to our own place—then perhaps we should pause to reevaluate our peacemaking paradigm. As Gandhi believed, we must first pursue nonviolence within.

As I draw this reflection to a close, I find myself unsettled by its sense of resolution. These final pages sound much too sure. Honestly, I have more

---

13. Martin Luther King, Jr. observed as much in his speech at Riverside Church in New York City on April 4, 1967, when he said, "I knew that I could never again raise my voice against the violence of the oppressed in the ghettos without having first spoken clearly to the greatest purveyor of violence in the world today—my own government." King was assassinated exactly one year after this making this speech on April 4, 1968. For the full speech, see Martin Luther King, Jr., "Beyond Vietnam—A Time to Break Silence," http://www.americanrhetoric.com/speeches/mlkatimetobreaksilence.htm.

questions now than when I began. Perhaps I have written with confidence because I want to convince myself. I *want* resolution. But it does not come. Nor should it. Echoing the German writer Rainer Maria Rilke, I suspect that if I embrace the questions, fully live into them, one day I may find myself living into some answers.[14] Because of the fluidity of this journey, I feel I cannot truly call myself a peacemaker, or perhaps even a Christian, for I never fully live out the profundity of these titles. Each day I betray them in some way. I believe in peace and in Christ insofar as I incarnate those beliefs. If I profess belief in peace but participate in acts of division, then in those moments, I do not really believe in peace. If I profess belief in the resurrection of Christ but ignore the hungry homeless person on the street, then in that moment, I do not truly believe in the power of resurrection. Our beliefs are not found primarily in what we espouse, but rather in what we do. They exist in our actions, and thus our pursuits of peacemaking, of resurrection, of Christian discipleship are never complete.

Though we often claim to have "converted," I doubt there can actually be a single, identifiable *moment* of conversion. Rather, conversion is a process. It is not an isolated experience, a one-time event. It is not simple or easy; it cannot be realized in an instant. Christianity is a struggle, not an epiphany. It is a journey, a Way of being in the world. This is why community is essential, to call us away from our settled assumptions and undisturbed prejudices and invite us to see with different lenses inside alternative frameworks. Thus, we are *daily* in the process of being converted, whether to Christianity, or peacemaking, or the journeys toward empathy and reconciliation. As my brother has often said, we are unfinished. I wonder, then, if such descriptions as *aspiring* Christian and *aspiring* peacemaker might be more appropriate.[15]

In these unfinished aspirations, however, many of us Christians tend to siphon all mystery from the divine, simplifying our perceptions of

14. Rilke, *Letters to a Young Poet*, 27.

15. I thank friend and author Peter Rollins for much of this thought process. Yet, even as I write the above, I am struck with the possibility that these observations may only have merit if coupled with the assumption that Christian discipleship, for example, entails perfect adherence to the Way of Jesus, and thus to fall short of this perfection, as the Apostle Paul indicates we have all done (Rom 3:23), requires a qualification of the term *Christian*: If we are not perfect in our Christianity, then we are not actually Christians, but rather aspiring to be so. But this realization confuses me because, at the time of this writing, I simultaneously resonate with the idea that conversion is a perpetual process, as well as the idea that Christianity does not necessitate perfection. Here lies a quintessential example of the contradictory nature of human fluidity.

biblical truth to single, uncontestable facts. We practice a kind of religious reductionism, or more specifically, a denominational reductionism, taking our inevitable identities within particular traditions and making them the only right identity for the world. Rather than pursuing a radical discipleship to the Way of Jesus, we place our allegiances under these umbrellas of denominational exclusivism. The sirens of contented salvation sing far too loudly for us to hear anything but our own anthems. Too many of us claiming Christianity cannot bring ourselves to remove our tinted lenses and, even if only for a moment, try to imagine the world outside of our own comfortable framework. In his fantastic book *Who Is My Enemy?*, ethicist and theologian Lee C. Camp discusses Miroslav Volf's call to "double vision"—that is, seeing things from the perspective of others, primarily from the perspective of our enemies. This practice can allow for our differing understandings of justice to be juxtaposed with each other so that they might sharpen one another. This is not, Camp points out, "intellectually lazy relativism," but rather he argues that we must reject both the modernist notion that we can "simply see things with timeless, universal eyes," as well as the perspective that all opinions are of equal quality or merit. Instead, practicing "double vision" is an attempt at "intellectual humility."[16]

Christian Zionism exemplifies the reductionist nature of dominant strands of Western Christianity, rejecting this intellectual humility and instead pledging their loyalty to an isolated interpretation of proof-texted biblical passages. (In all honesty, advocates of nonviolence have often done the same thing.) Rather than stepping back and seeing the complex threads of justice, mercy, compassion, and love woven throughout the scriptural narratives, Christian Zionists especially cling to decontextualized readings of Old Testament prophecy and Revelation, meanwhile avoiding in my mind Jesus's socio-political relevance by sweeping him into a convenient, unthreatening box labeled "spiritual." In my experience, many Christian Zionists refuse to entertain even the *possibility* of other interpretations of biblical narratives, but rather hold to the proverbial script of their group-think. To illustrate, in a conversation I had with one Christian Zionist about issues in Israel and Palestine, the individual actually ventured so far as to acknowledge the oppression of the Palestinian people and confess that it was indeed terrible, but then quickly added, "But the ways of God are mysterious. Who are we to question those ways?" Others have pointed out

16. Camp, *Who Is My Enemy?*, 7.

to me that God used the Hebrew people to wipe out the indigenous population long ago with Joshua, so why can't God do it again?

I will be candid: If our theology is one of a God who will commit multiple genocides because of preference for a particular people, then we need a new theology. If our theology is one that excuses occupation and oppression because we dare not question the methods of a transcendent God, then we need a new theology. We need a theology that is consistent with the biblical revelation that "God does not show favoritism" (Acts 10:34).[17] We need a theology that does not exalt prophecy over incarnation. I remember hearing friend and author David Dark once say, "We cannot use the Old Testament to avoid the lordship of Jesus." Jesus spent his time with the poor and marginalized of his day. If our theology does not lead us to the same places, I fear we are terribly off course.

I cannot help but believe that God wants to use us, in all our unfinished and broken pieces, to change the world, no matter how small or humbling such pursuits may be. I resonate with the belief of sixteenth-century monastic and mystic Teresa of Avila that God has no hands, no feet, no body on earth but ours. Yet, I proceed with caution, careful to avoid Southern preacher and idol-crasher Will Campbell's notion of the "idolatry of heroism."[18] I do not want to be so vain as to believe I am the savior or the champion, that I will usher in the climax of anyone's story. I hear again the words of Oscar Romero: "We are workers, not master builders, ministers, not messiahs. We are prophets of a future not our own." We will not always see the changes we are striving for, but immediate transformation is not the call.

Considering the biblical phrase "you shall know them by their fruit" proves illustrative. "Fruit does not emerge in a single day," Lederach observes, "nor is it isolated from a context of soils, roots, and climate. It takes time . . . "[19] In order to produce good fruit, whether literally or metaphorically, we must be willing to get dirt under our fingernails, digging our hands into the soil of a place, into its historical context and shared memories. When planting the seeds that may eventually bear fruit, we cannot expect to taste the results quickly or without diligent attention to the growing

17. Although, liberation theology counsels us that God does in fact practice partiality, and it is toward the poor and oppressed, with whom the God of liberation stands. See Gutiérrez, *A Theology of Liberation*.

18. Campbell and Goode, ed., *And the Criminals With Him*, 12. For more on Will Campbell, see Campbell and Goode, *Crashing the Idols*.

19. Lederach, *The Moral Imagination*, 57.

process. We must prune, water, and fertilize our sapling, often even for years, before the first fruits emerge. In many ways, the art of planting is woven with risk and trust. It embraces both the possibility of failure and the hope of tradition. Thus, the call of peace praxis is to be part of the good, long work of justice and reconciliation, learning the stories of people and their places, and then embracing presence with those who suffer—that is, striving simply to *be*. Toward the end of my stay in Hebron, my teammate Rosie emailed me this quote she attributed to Henri Nouwen: "The friend who can be silent with us in a moment of despair or confusion, who can stay with us in an hour of grief and bereavement, who can tolerate not knowing . . . not healing, not curing . . . that is a friend who cares." Wherever we find those suffering, those who experience the world "from below," we must humble ourselves to experience presence with them.

Often, attempting to pigeonhole me under a "pro-Palestinian" label (meaning to the exclusion of Israeli concerns or grievances), people ask me, "What would you do if the tables suddenly turned, and the *Palestinians* had all the power and began oppressing and occupying the Israelis?" I simply reply, "I suppose I'd work in Tel Aviv." My support of the Palestinians does not stem from an arbitrary opposition to Israelis, but rather from a conviction to be on the side of the oppressed. Besides, peacemaking in Israel and Palestine is not just "helping the Palestinians." Peacemaking is a dual liberation, as it seeks to liberate the oppressed from being oppressed and the oppressors from being oppressors. Israel needs as much liberation from the occupation as Palestine. Following the final line of a Wendell Berry poem, our task is to "practice resurrection," creating cultures of life in the midst of cultures of death, reconstructing out of the rubble of destruction, in hopes of witnessing blossoms sprouting from the branches of dying trees.[20]

As I move forward, then, in pursuit of nonviolence and the hard work of peacemaking, I echo the words of Gandhi: "In the secret of my heart I am in perpetual quarrel with God that He should allow such things [as the occupation, e.g.] to go on. My nonviolence seems almost impotent. But the answer comes at the end of the daily quarrel that . . . impotence is in men. *I must try on without losing faith even though I may break in the attempt.*"[21] But what happens if we do break? How can we hope to sustain ourselves and remain true to the difficult work before us? In a world broken in shambles, with evil manifest in the rampant chaos of senseless hatred,

---

20. Berry, *The Selected Poems of Wendell Berry*, 88.
21. Merton, *Gandhi on Non-Violence*, 89, emphasis mine.

no resolution or transformation in sight, how can we possibly hope to be peaceable? My friend Richard Goode suggests a way: "Together, Brother McRay. Together."

Thanks be to God.

Michael McRay
Nashville, Tennessee | Belfast, Northern Ireland
May-December 2012

Bibliography

Berry, Wendell. *The Selected Poems of Wendell Berry.* Washington, DC: Counterpoint, 1998.

———. *Sex, Economy, Freedom, and Community: Eight Essays.* New York: Pantheon, 1993.

Boesak, Allan, and Curtiss Paul DeYoung. *Radical Reconciliation: Beyond Political Pietism and Christian Quietism.* Maryknoll, NY: Orbis, 2012.

Bonhoeffer, Dietrich. *Letters and Papers from Prison.* New York: Touchstone, 1997.

B'Tselem. "Separation Barrier." No pages. Online: http://www.btselem.org/separation_barrier/map.

———. "Separation Barrier: Statistics." No pages. Online: http://www.btselem.org/separation_barrier/statistics.

———. "Water crisis: International Law and the Water Crisis in the Occupied Territories." No pages. Online: http://www.btselem.org/water/international_law.

———. "Water crisis: Statistics." No pages. Online: http://www.btselem.org/water/statistics.

Camp, Lee C. *Who Is My Enemy? Questions American Christians Must Face About Islam – And Themselves.* Grand Rapids: Brazos Press, 2011.

Campbell, Will D. *Writings on Reconciliation and Resistance.* Eugene, OR: Cascade, 2010.

Campbell, Will D., and Richard C. Goode. *Crashing the Idols: The Vocation of Will D. Campbell (and Any Other Christian for That Matter).* Eugene, OR: Cascade, 2011.

Campbell, Will D., and Richard C. Goode, eds. *And the Criminals With Him: Essays in Honor of Will D. Campbell and All the Reconciled.* Eugene, OR: Cascade, 2012.

Carey, Roane, and Jonathan Shainin, eds. *The Other Israel: Voices of Refusal and Dissent.* New York: New Press, 2002.

Claiborne, Shane, and Jonathan Wilson-Hartgrove. *Becoming the Answer to Our Prayers: Prayer for Ordinary Radicals.* Downers Grove, IL: InterVarsity, 2008.

Gutiérrez, Gustavo. *A Theology of Liberation: History, Politics, and Salvation.* London: SCM, 2001.

Halpern, Jodi, and Harvey M. Weinstein. "Rehumanizing the Other: Empathy and Reconciliation." *Human Rights Quarterly* 26 (2004) 561–83.

Hatch, Jonathan R. "Separation Barriers and Idolatry: Examining Physically-Reinforced Segregation in Belfast through a Theological Lens." Lecture, Irish School of Ecumenics (Trinity College Dublin), Belfast, Northern Ireland, December 6, 2012.

Lederach, John Paul. *The Moral Imagination: The Art and Soul of Building Peace.* New York: Oxford University Press, 2005.

McRay, Jonathan. *You Have Heard It Said: Events of Reconciliation.* Eugene, OR: Resource Publications, 2011.

Merton, Thomas, ed. *Gandhi on Non-Violence.* New York: New Directions, 2007.

ReMillard, Francis M. *Is Israel an Apartheid State?* Pamphlet, Chapel Hill: Israeli Commitee Against House Demolitions-USA, 2009.

Rilke, Rainer Maria. *Letters to a Young Poet.* London: Norton, 1993.

Sabbagh, Karl. *Palestine: History of a Lost Nation.* New York: Grove, 2006.

Zehr, Howard. *The Little Book of Restorative Justice.* Intercourse, PA: Good Books, 2002.

Zinn, Howard. *A People's History of the United States, Volume 1: America's Beginnings to Reconstruction.* New York: New Press, 2003.

Contributors

Lee C. Camp, Professor of Theology & Ethics at Lipscomb University in Nashville, Tennessee, as well as the creator and host of the Tokens Show (www.TokensShow.com). He is the author of *Mere Discipleship: Radical Christianity in a Rebellious World* and *Who Is My Enemy? Questions American Christians Must Face About Islam and Themselves.*

Jonathan McRay, worked with the Al Basma Center in Beit Sahour from 2009 to 2010. He has also worked as a journalist and nonviolent activist in Israel and Palestine and is the author of *You Have Heard It Said: Events of Reconciliation* (2011). He has a BA in English Literature and Language and is currently pursuing graduate work in conflict transformation and restorative justice with the Center for Justice and Peacebuilding at Eastern Mennonite University in Harrisonburg, Virginia.

Acknowledgements

As with any book, having one author's name on the cover is somewhat deceitful since no work is truly done alone. We are not islands. I owe both my musings and my opportunities to all those I've encountered who have shaped my direction. First and foremost, I offer my humblest and most heartfelt gratitude to my parents, David and Joan. Without their expressed support, clear dedication, intentional love, and endless generosity, none of the preceding pages would exist. To my paternal grandparents, John and Annette, I extend sincere thanks for their selfless hospitality, particularly over the last year, and especially to my grandmother, whose morning conversations over coffee and homemade muffins provided me with much fertile soil in which to plant many of my final reflections. Additionally, I thank my uncle, Rob McRay, for organizing the collection of funds donated for this trip, as well as all those who generously gave their money to make this experience (and thus book) possible: my maternal grandparents Joe and Rosalyn Wilkerson, as well as Ruth and Frank Balch, Mike Duncan, Quinton and Jacqueline Dickerson, Marolyn and Louie Woodall, Jere and Evon Lee, Jackie Bradford, and Richard and Carolyn Batey.

Furthermore, with all sincerity, I thank the following: Alexa LeBouef, for being a soundboard for me when putting the finishing touches on the book and for her gracious support and encouragement along every step of our journey thus far; Richard Goode, who not only first introduced me to the work of Christian Peacemaker Teams, but whose classroom teaching, mentorship, and friendship have informed my understanding and practice of Christian discipleship as much as anyone else in my life; Lee Camp, for his generous assistance with publishing ventures and writing the foreword, as well as his instruction on the nonviolent teachings of Jesus and the practice of radical discipleship; my brother John, for his essay on Al Basma at the end of this book, and whose talent for words and critical thought was much appreciated when editing my preface and epilogue; my sister Anna, whose love and endless encouragement deserves countless blessings; all those who graciously endorsed this book; Maria Harrison, who helped cement my love of and sharpen my skill for writing; my CPT teammates, Kathy, Rosie, Jean, Chris, and Carrie; Tarek Abuata and all those in CPT who granted me the internship and offered their support for the project; Ron Sider, for his speech in 1984 that inspired the creation of CPT; Abu and Um Shadi for their hospitality in allowing me to use their "paradise" in Beit Sahour as a sanctuary during my stint in Hebron; Mahmoud and all my friends in Israel and Palestine who greet me with "*Ahlan wasahlan*"; the members of my dad's medical group, Paul McClung, Allyson Cook, Dwight and Katie Willett, Mike Richardson, and Heather Holmes; all those in our contemplative group at Riverbend prison, for their conversation and community: Ed McKeown, Jorge Sanjines, Tony Vick, Chris Hallum, Nathan "Slick" Miller, Mike "Fuzy" Waldron, Craig "Dusty" Katzenmiller, Ben Oliver, Lenae Chambers, Forrest and Valerie Busler, Joshua McArthur, Joanna Bradley, Bruce Morrill, Richard Goode, Grant Winter, Andrew Krinks, and Alexa LeBouef; Ragnhild Esbensen, for her wise advice in revising sections of the epilogue; and a special thank you to all those who took the time to respond to these letters from "Apartheid Street": Steve Greek, my uncle Barry McRay, Sandra Stidham, Tarek, my aunt Lisa Ramsay, Andrew Shankles, Jonathon Valentin, John, Anna, Jake Burton, Evon Lee, Becky Smith, Rosie, Zac Swann, Urszula Collier, Carolyn Batey, Jil Jennewein, my grandmother Annette, my parents, Alexa, Bruce Morrill, Richard, Lee, Derek Brown, my uncle Rob, Kathy, and Neil Christy.

Finally, I offer my thanks to Rodney Clapp, Jim Tedrick, Christian Amondson, Heather Carraher, and all the staff at Wipf and Stock Publishers.

Glossary

Ahlan wasahlan – A Palestinian professor and author in Qalqiliya instructed me of the phrase's origin and meaning. Transliterated as *"halalta ahlan watïeta sahlan,"* it essentially means "you are received as part of my family, and your path is now easy, as if moving across a plain."

Green Line – The only internationally recognized border between Israel and the West Bank. It refers to the armistice line established between Israel and the Jordanian-occupied "west bank" of the Jordan River between 1949 and 1967. When Israel won the Six Day War in June 1967, they claimed the West Bank from Jordan and have occupied it since. Thus, the Green Line is often referred to as the "1967 borders."

Gutnick Center – Settler-run center in Hebron near the Ibrahimi Mosque.

Intifada – Literally in Arabic, "shaking off." Refers to two Palestinian uprisings against the Israeli occupation. The First *Intifada* took place between 1987 and 1993, and the Second *Intifada* from late 2000 until approximately 2005.

Keffiyeh – A traditional head covering for Arab men. Due in large part to the fashion decision of former Palestinian political leader Yasser Arafat, the *keffiyeh* has become a symbol of Palestinian nationalism and solidarity.

Knesset – The Israeli parliament.

Nakba – Arabic for "catastrophe." It refers to the displacement of more than 750,000 Palestinians in 1948 to make way for the creation of the new State of Israel.

Qalandia – The checkpoint between Jerusalem and Ramallah.

Settlement – Israeli Jewish housing projects, towns, or cities built on land occupied since 1967, i.e., in the West Bank, Gaza, or East Jerusalem.

Shebaab – Palestinian young men, usually between the ages of sixteen and forty.

Shuhada Street – Referenced on the map as Al Shohada Street. Formerly one of Hebron's busiest streets, it is now closed to Palestinians, and thus is called "Apartheid Street" by the local Palestinians.

Sumoud – Arabic for "steadfastness"

APPENDIX A

Further Reading

Israeli-Palestinian Conflict

Academic

Berry, Mike, and Greg Philo. *Israel and Palestine: Competing Histories.* Ann Arbor, MI: Pluto, 2006.

Finkelstein, Norman G. *Image and Reality of the Israel-Palestine Conflict,* 2nd ed. New York: Verso, 2001.

Karmi, Ghada. *Married to Another Man: Israel's Dilemma in Palestine.* Ann Arbor, MI: Pluto, 2007.

Khalidi, Rashid. *The Iron Cage: The Story of the Palestinian Struggle for Statehood.* Boston: Beacon, 2007.

Makdisi, Saree. *Palestine Inside Out: An Everday Occupation.* New York: Norton, 2008.

Mearsheimer, John J., and Stephen M. Walt. *The Israel Lobby and U.S. Foreign Policy.* New York: Farrar, Straus and Giroux, 2007.

Morris, Benny. *Righteous Victims: A History of the Zionist-Arab Conflict, 1881-2001,* 2nd. ed. New York: Vintage, 2001.

Pappe, Ilan. *The Ethnic Cleansing of Palestine.* Oxford: Oneworld, 2006.

Said, Edward. *The Question of Palestine.* New York: Vintage, 1992.

Stories

Abuelaish, Izzeldin. *I Shall Not Hate: A Gaza Doctor's Journey on the Road to Peace and Human Dignity.* New York: Walker & Company, 2010.

Al Jundi, Sami, and Jen Marlowe. *The Hour of Sunlight: One Palestinian's Journey from Prisoner to Peacemaker.* New York: Nation, 2011.

Barghouti, Mourid. *I Saw Ramallah.* New York: Anchor, 2000.

Chacour, Elias, and David Hazard. *Blood Brothers.* Tarrytown, NY: Chosen, 1984

Chacour, Elias. *Faith Beyond Despair: Building Hope in the Holy Land.* London: Canterbury Press Norwich, 2008.

———. *We Belong to the Land: The Story of a Palestinian Israeli Who Lives for Peace and Reconciliation.* Notre Dame: University of Notre Dame Press, 2001.

Nusseibeh, Sari, Anthony David. *Once Upon a Country: A Palestinian Life.* New York: Farrar, Straus and Giroux, 2007.

Pearlman, Wendy. *Occupied Voices: Stories of Everyday Life from the Second Intifada.* New York: Thunder's Mouth/Nation, 2003.

Shehadeh, Raja. *Occupation Diaries.* London: Profile, 2012.

———. *Palestinian Walks: Forays Into a Vanishing Landscape.* New York: Scribner, 2007.

———. *Strangers in the House: Coming of Age in Occupied Palestine.* New York: Penguin, 2003.

———. *When the Birds Stopped Singing: Life in Ramallah Under Siege.* South Royalton, VT: Steerforth, 2003.

Sultan, Cathy. *Israeli and Palestinian Voices: A Dialogue with Both Sides,* 2nd ed. Minneapolis: Scarletta, 2006.

Peacemaking, Nonviolence, and Reconciliation

Boesak, Allan, and Curtiss Paul DeYoung. *Radical Reconciliation: Beyond Political Pietism and Christian Quietism.* Maryknoll, NY: Orbis, 2012.

Brimlow, Robert. *What About Hitler?: Wrestling with Jesus' Call to Nonviolence in an Evil World.* Grand Rapids: Brazos, 2006.

Camp, Lee. *Who Is My Enemy? Questions American Christians Must Face About Islam— and Themselves.* Grand Rapids: Brazos, 2011.

Lederach, John Paul. *Building Peace: Sustainable Reconciliation in Divided Societies.* Washington, DC: United States Institute of Peace, 1997.

———. *The Moral Imagination: The Art and Soul of Building Peace.* New York: Oxford University Press, 2005.

Lederach, John Paul, and Angela Jill Lederach. *When Blood and Bones Cry Out: Journeys Through the Soundscape of Healing and Reconciliation.* New York: Oxford University Press, 2010.

McRay, Jonathan. *You Have Heard It Said: Events of Reconciliation.* Eugene, OR: Resource Publications, 2011.

Merton, Thomas, ed. *Gandhi on Non-Violence.* New York: New Directions, 2007.

Wink, Walter. *Jesus and Nonviolence: A Third Way.* Minneapolis: Fortress, 2003.

APPENDIX B

Al Basma Center for the Developmentally Disabled
Where Part of Your Money Is Going

IN ORDER TO GIVE *you, the reader, an understanding of where 25 percent of royalties has gone, I asked my brother Jonathan to write an essay describing the beauty of the place that is Al Basma. To make further donations, please contact albasmapalestine@gmail.com:*

The Al Basma Center is a restorative place for people with developmental disabilities in the village of Beit Sahour, the "House of Vigilance." This ancient village is located in a valley on the eastern side of Bethlehem, between the hills rising to Jerusalem and the desert of the Jordan Valley. Started in 1987, Al Basma (which means "the smile" in Arabic) had almost no funds and no tables or chairs, and so the six students sat on the floor. Now, thirty students walk or ride a small bus to a stone building where the edge of town begins to fade. They still have few funds, but their creative programs now include olivewood carving, homemade fuel from olivewood sawdust to heat the center in winter, recycling paper and making Christmas cards, weaving on traditional looms, drama and exercise, speech therapy and hygiene classes, and a greenhouse with one of the first aquaponics systems[1] in Palestine. The students cultivate practical and artistic skills and the belief that they are vital members and contributors to their community.

---

1. Aquaponics is a symbiotic food production system that hybridizes traditional aquaculture (raising aquatic animals in tanks) and hydroponics (plant cultivation in water) in a closed-loop system so that wastewater from the fish is cycled to the plants, where it is cleansed and recirculated to the fish.

Six women are the leaders and teachers and, like the students, half are Muslims and half Christians. These women sometimes sacrifice their paltry pay so the Center can continue each month. The days are filled with good work, with laughter and explosive arguments and then laughter again. The work tables are transformed into banquet tables where they eat meager vegetarian feasts because meat is too expensive. And then they remove the tables at the end of each day and dance to Arabic pop music between the pink walls. The next day, this ceremony begins again.

Farmer and poet Wendell Berry writes that, "The real work of planet-saving will be small, humble, and humbling, and (insofar as it involves love) pleasing and rewarding. Its jobs will be too many to count, too many to report, too many to be publicly noticed or rewarded, too small to make anyone rich or famous."[2] He doesn't know it, but he is writing about Al Basma.

Jonathan McRay

---

2. Berry, *Sex, Economy, Freedom, and Community*, 24.

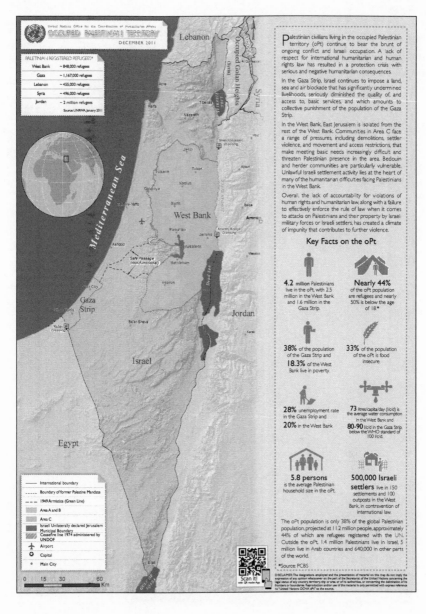

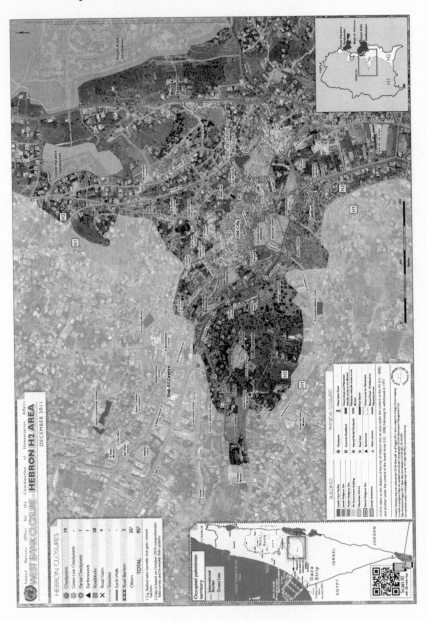

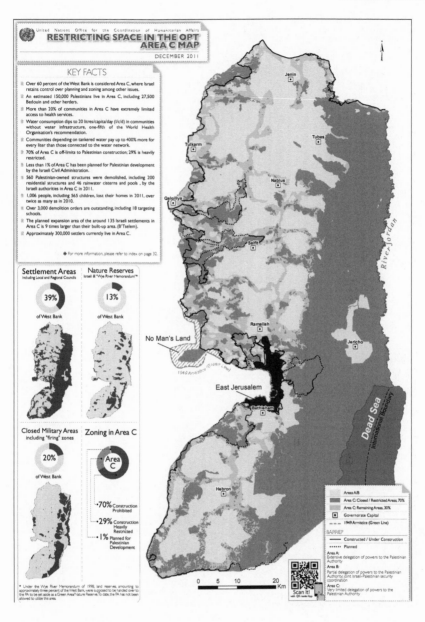

Printed in Great Britain
by Amazon.co.uk, Ltd.,
Marston Gate.